THE
TREACHEROUS PATH

THE
TREACHEROUS
PATH

VLADIMIR YAKUNIN

Biteback Publishing

First published in Great Britain in 2018 by
Biteback Publishing Ltd
Westminster Tower
3 Albert Embankment
London SE1 7SP
Copyright © Vladimir Yakunin 2018

ISBN 978-1-78590-301-4

10 9 8 7 6 5 4 3 2 1

A CIP catalogue record for this book is available from the British Library.

Set in Adobe Caslon Pro

Printed and bound in Great Britain by
CPI Group (UK) Ltd, Croydon CR0 4YY

MIX
Paper from
responsible sources
FSC
www.fsc.org   FSC® C020471

I wish to dedicate this book to my wife Natalia, and to my sons and family. They have always been at my side, during both good times and bad.

'The world perishes not from bandits and fires, but from hatred, hostility and all these petty squabbles.'

– Anton Chekhov, *Uncle Vanya*

CONTENTS

FOREWORD

I t is sometimes argued that ten different things can be said about Russia and all of them can be true. Russia as a country is a complex phenomenon, with different histories, cultural patterns and political orientations. This does not mean that relativism rules. Far from it. The lived experiences of Russians can be fundamentally divergent, but they are united in some sort of common endeavour and an appreciation of different aspects of the truth. This is why accounts provided by people who have been part of that contradictory reality are so important. There have been surprisingly few memoirs from the present generation of leaders and public personalities. While the Mikhail Gorbachev period from the mid-1980s has been covered by numerous memoirs, and the Boris Yeltsin years in the 1990s has been written about extensively, there is much to learn about the years since Vladimir Putin came to office in 2000 – which is why this personal testimony from Vladimir Yakunin is so welcome.

The book provides a profound insight into the realities of Russia today, as told by one of the makers of modern Russia.

Yakunin's life story mirrors that of Russia itself over the past few decades. Born in 1948 in the Vladimir region, he lived until he was fourteen in Estonia, before his family moved to Leningrad (now St Petersburg), the city that he considers his hometown. In 1972, Yakunin graduated from the Leningrad Mechanical Institute, and then began his diverse and impressive career. He worked in the State Institute for Applied Chemistry, followed by two years compulsory military service in the Soviet Army. After demobilisation in 1977, he worked as a senior engineer in the State Committee for International Trade of the Council of Ministers, and then headed the Foreign Relations Department of the Ioffe Physico-Technical Institute. He was invited by KGB agents to work with them, and in 1985 he and his family left for New York to join the Soviet diplomatic mission at the United Nations.

Yakunin powerfully describes the double life in New York (as a diplomat and an agent) and the enormous stress that this produced, as well as the powerful impressions the country made on him – impressions which informed the work of the Dialogue of Civilizations, the social movement that Yakunin co-founded in the early 2000s.

Like Putin, Yakunin was out of the country when Gorbachev's *perestroika* (restructuring) transformed the Soviet Union. By 1989 the cold war was effectively over and the Communist system had been dissolved. In its place came an ill-formed democracy and a thoroughly disorganised economy. The entrepreneurial energies of the country were unleashed, although much of this took semi-criminal if not outright bandit forms. Yakunin shares the view of much of the enlightened elite of the times that the Soviet Union had been running out of steam and that change was necessary, but he also shares the view that the ill-thought-out reforms ultimately destroyed the country and catastrophically undermined its position in the world.

Yakunin returned to St Petersburg in early 1991, just as the USSR entered its final trajectory towards disintegration. He describes the gangster capitalism of that decade and the emergence of powerful oligarchs who effectively tried to take over the state.

Although the period was lawless and the economy lacked an adequate regulatory framework, the opportunities for active people were enormous, and Yakunin's account provides a vivid insight into this period of the 'primitive accumulation of capital', as Marx described the early stages of capitalist development. It was in this period that he got to know Putin.

In 1997, Putin, by now working in the Kremlin, invited Yakunin to return to state service as the head of the Northwest Regional branch of the State Inspectorate, a post he held until December 2000. Yakunin took over the supervision of the major port development at Ust-Luga and he writes vividly of the herculean task of building a major seaport, effectively from scratch, and the economic and geopolitical imperatives driving the project. He describes how the private sector was brought in to work in partnership with the state to turn the development of the port into a major Russian success story.

This discussion also reveals some of the major dividing lines in Russian debates over economic policy. Yakunin clearly believes that the state has a major part to play in economic development, but at the same time argues that industrial policy should be based on market methods of regulation and competitiveness. This is the classic Putinite formulation, although Yakunin is critical of the policies pursued in recent years. He treads a path between those advocating Soviet-style mobilisational forms of development, and neoliberals on the other flank who believe in the magic properties of the untrammelled market.

Between December 2000 and February 2002 Yakunin served as deputy transport minister under Sergei Frank, giving him the opportunity to put his ideas into practice while at the same time travelling all over the country, with responsibilities for merchant fleet and seaport development. In October 2003, Yakunin was appointed deputy head of the new Russian Railways corporation, and in June 2005 became its head, a position he held until August 2015.

Yakunin describes the challenges of modernising the system, including the need to attract private capital while not allowing the system to become fragmented. The privatisation and fragmentation of British Railways by the John Major government in the early 1990s is held up as an example of how not to do things. Yakunin describes the achievements of his tenure in office, including the creation of the high-speed line between Moscow and St Petersburg, with the Sapsan network reducing the journey time from overnight to four hours. The Trans-Siberian and Baikal-Amur Mainline (BAM) are also being upgraded, accompanied by a massive programme of rolling stock and engine renewal. Another herculean project was building the transport infrastructure for the Sochi Winter Olympic games of February 2014. The combined road and rail project running up from the coast at Adler all the way up the steep river valley, much of it on bridges and through tunnels, to the ski slopes of Krasnaya Polyana is one of the great engineering achievements of our time.

Everyone who sees the swooping bridges, handsome stations, elegant tunnel entrances, humming electrical substations, and smooth roads stands in awe.

Yakunin does not hide the storm clouds gathering over the recent period of Russian politics. His own resignation as head of Russian Railways in 2015 has been interpreted as part of some dark intrigue, whereas in fact Yakunin argues it was prompted above all by the tightening budget restrictions on investment, and what he considered the ill-advised move to freeze railway tariffs in 2014, starving Russian Railways of investment resources. His final period in office was also accompanied by systematic attempts to denigrate his achievements and even his abilities, and he was placed on the US sanctions list (meaning that he cannot travel to the US). This sad turn of events, effectively a shift to something akin to a new cold war, after all the bright hopes of earlier years, imbues the final parts of this book with a pessimistic tone.

This is balanced, however, by the continued commitment to the Dialogue of Civilizations project, bringing together public intellectuals, religious and civil society leaders, politicians and academics to discuss problems of civilisational identity, cultural autonomy, diverse paths of development and above all, dialogue as a method of political and social engagement. In 2016 this work became more formalised though the establishment of the Dialogue of Civilizations Research Institute based in Berlin.

This brief survey indicates how Yakunin has been at the intersection of the main debates and developments of modern Russian history. Like so many others, he had hoped to salvage a better and more humane version of the Soviet Union, and then in the post-Communist years became committed to Russia's development as a market democracy, although with a statist inflection. He makes no secret of his support for Putin, who in his eyes – and the eyes of so many other Russians – saved the country from the threat of going the way of the Soviet Union by restoring state capacity, elements of stability, rational governance, and maintaining Russia's status in the world. This does not mean that there are no disagreements, especially over economic policy and governance issues, but there are now institutions in which such discussions can be held.

Equally, Yakunin's account shows the importance of what could be called the 'spiritual' side of national development and international cooperation. The discussions in the framework of the Dialogue of Civilizations, as I can personally attest, have been accompanied by a commitment to fundamental human values. While there is sharp critique of the perceived false universalism of much of contemporary left-liberal identity thinking, of globalisation as a model of human development if it threatens national cultures and diverse histories, and of the assertion that the liberal international order is synonymous with order itself, these debates are essential if humane and pluralistic forms of international and inter-civilisation dialogue are to survive. It is in this spirit that Yakunin's book is written, and his moving personal testimony is essential reading for anyone trying to understand Russia today.

Richard Sakwa
University of Kent

CHAPTER ONE

THE TRUTH IS NEVER BLACK AND WHITE

They say that there are two sides to every story; I think perhaps that it is more complex than that. After all, a lot of stories have been told about me. For instance that I am merciless, the kind of man who eats other people for breakfast, bones and all. That I am part of a secret cabal of former KGB officers who have plotted to take control of the country; that I am an agent of the Kremlin; that I am a devoted Orthodox Christian; that I was one of the country's most powerful men before I fell from grace (the list is endless) – but only some of these stories are true. By the same token, many myths have come to circulate about Russia – that it was saved in the '90s by the actions of liberal reformers; that it is an authoritarian state which has banished free speech; that we all long secretly for the return of the Soviet empire – and, again, few have any basis in reality. This book will tell a different kind of story, not just about the life of a single citizen, but also, I hope, about the experiences of an entire nation.

Over the past seventy years, I have led many lives, and so, over the same period, has Russia. I have been a scientist, an intelligence officer, a diplomat, an entrepreneur, a government minister and, finally, the president of Russian Railways – RZD (Rossiiskie Zheleznye Dorogi, literally Russian Iron Roads) – one of the largest transportation companies in the world. When I was born, Russia was at the centre of the Soviet Union, one of the earth's two superpowers. I saw it grow and change and decline, before I was forced to watch as the positive energy that had animated perestroika surged out of control and demolished the institutions it had been intended to save. I looked on with sorrow as the country floundered for over a decade – as its economy, its entire civic life crumbled, even as some of the country's most energetic citizens grasped enthusiastically at the opportunities the new polity offered – until eventually something approaching stability was achieved.

It has been a time of convulsion, of tectonic changes that have altered every element of society's existence, sending shockwaves right through the world. I have witnessed the corruption of the Soviet *nomenklatura* and the savage lawlessness of the new breed of businessmen who came to prominence after 1991. I have watched, helpless, as, in the years of chaos and want, my family (like so many millions of others) was afflicted by the breakdown of our nation's infrastructure. But though I have never considered myself to be a politician grabbing after power (politics is a game of blood, war and inequality; I have always tried to keep my distance), I have been more than a mute observer, never crouching idly in a corner.

As a field officer in the KGB, my life was dedicated to preserving the fabric of a society that at the time I believed was the

THE TRUTH IS NEVER BLACK AND WHITE

surest guarantor of peace, equality and freedom throughout the world; and since the fall of communism I have played a part in rebuilding a nation that for a long time seemed to have been buried deep in the debris of the old order. Out of the mud and swamps of the Baltic coast I oversaw the construction of a crucial plank in Russia's new economy, and I know what it is like to be responsible for the fate of over a million employees and to control a transport network that reaches into every corner of the world's largest country. So if I have been shaped by the times I have lived through – and I want in this book to show how the things I have seen and done have moulded my personality and redirected the way my thoughts flow – I have also, I hope, left my own mark on them.

Many books have been written about my country in the last few years. Some are well-researched, exhaustively sourced and elegantly told, but they all are the work of outsiders. Their writers have watched and listened and written, but they have not taken part. I have. This is the first record of my country's recent history to be written by someone with such an intimate knowledge of its government and the key personalities within it. It is an insider's story, one that offers an unashamedly subjective perspective, which is markedly different to the accounts that you might have become accustomed to reading in your newspaper or watching on your TV screens. It is a perspective that I feel has been sorely lacking in much, if not all, of the discourse about Russia that takes place in the West. In my experience, the majority of people living in Britain or the United States tend to regard my country in oversimplified, almost Manichaean terms, but the truth is never black and white.

I also wanted to write this book to allow me to reflect and take stock of the tumultuous events of the past decades, and the closing of a significant chapter in my life has provided me with the opportunity to do so. In August 2015, I retired from my position at the helm of Russian Railways, a post I had held for ten eventful years (a period preceded by four years as first deputy Minister of the Railways and first deputy president of the state-owned company we formed to replace it). I managed its reformation from a ministry into a state-owned company, and over the same period witnessed the transformation of Russia itself. When I was made CEO of the newly constituted Russian Railways company in 2005, I was charged by President Vladimir Putin with the daunting task of overseeing its reform as well as undertaking the modernisation of a railway network comprising over 85,000km of track. In the process I also witnessed the arguments within Russia's elite about the direction our country should be taking; becoming an unwilling participant in many of the power struggles that played out within the state, and seeing at first hand how supposedly neutral entities such as law enforcement or environmental agencies could be used as pawns in political games.

Of course, as soon as my departure was announced, newspapers across the world filled up with idle, mendacious criticism and innuendo. My family, my home, my friends; everything and everyone in my life seemed to be fair game. Even now, if you google my name you will mostly find reams of speculation and rumour; in this book I want to tell you a much more interesting story.

You will perhaps not like everything I have to say, and some of it will surprise you, but if you want to understand why Russia acts like it does, or why Russians think like they do, then this

4

book will be a good place to start. If nothing else, I want readers to at least begin to interrogate some of the opinions they
currently hold about my country. I do not do this because I am
animated by a blind nationalism, or from a pugnacious desire for
an argument, or because I am some kind of Kremlin stooge (to
do so would simultaneously make me a hypocrite and insult your
intelligence), but because I believe that we live in times imper-
illed by a fatal lack of understanding between the world's leading
nations. A profound danger that, it seems to me, is only made
more severe by the reluctance on the part of all the participants
to enter into any form of mutual dialogue. I am aware of how
this book might be received in the West, and yet still my modest
hope is that these words will go some way to ameliorating that
situation.

I sometimes get the feeling that many in the West think
that Europe ends at the borders of Belarus and Ukraine, and that
what lies beyond those lines is an unrecognisably strange land.
The kind of territory that on the maps made many hundreds of
years ago would have borne the motto: 'Here Be Dragons'. It
is an odd way of thinking about a nation that has for centuries
played a central part in the history of Europe, combining this
with its role as a bridge between East and West. (I see Russia
as a European nation, but not necessarily a Westernised one.)
But to many in the United Kingdom – perhaps since the days
of the 'Great Game' over a hundred years ago – Russia has been
wreathed in layers of myth and misapprehension (Winston
Churchill said of it that 'It is a riddle, wrapped in a mystery,
inside an enigma', and sometimes it seems as if there are many in
the West who still believe this to be true).

Of course, like all other nations on the planet, there are things we say or do that are incomprehensible or confusing even to our near neighbours. Some of these tics have been thousands of years in the making, while others are the result of more recent events in our history. Along with many thousands of my generation I have retained, for instance, the habit of thinking of almost every endeavour in which I am involved as a collective activity – so much so that when we recount the events we still habitually prefer to avoid using the pronoun 'I'. We were brought up in a world infused with this ethos – socialist values were embedded into almost every public interaction. (I am after all a product of the Soviet Union; I know that many consider me obsolete. Whether this is something to be mourned or mocked I leave to you to decide.)

But then at the same time, my experiences of, and relationship to, the political system that governed Russia and much of Eastern Europe for almost three quarters of a century are radically different to those of my sons, just as they will have a very different perspective on this era to someone born after 1991. I would never assume that all Britons, for instance, thought the same way; that age or class or geography or economics did not have important roles to play in ensuring that the United Kingdom was home to a kaleidoscope of different perspectives and opinions. Russia is no different. Indeed, I wonder whether its gargantuan scale, its dizzying ethnic and religious diversity, might make it even harder to generalise about what a 'typical' Russian outlook on the world might be.

If there is anything, however, that does perhaps set us apart it is that we are still, to a great extent, grappling with the consequences of the fall of the USSR. Those of us who had grown up as proud citizens of a superpower (even if we were well aware of its many flaws), whose heads had been filled with stories of the advances and glories of the Soviet regime, spent the '90s living in a land we barely recognised.

We were told we had liberty, but for most people this counted for little when they were poorer than they had ever been. I was more fortunate, but hated seeing our prestige and influence diminish. After the dissolution of the Soviet Union, Americans came to visit full of polite words and kind smiles, but we knew they saw us as citizens of a defeated country. Our living standards had been demolished, our history was being repudiated before our eyes, and we were being treated as an impotent second-class nation whose opinion no longer mattered.

This sense of loss and hurt, which left many people looking back fondly on the Communist era, has never been truly appreciated by other nations. Do not mistake me; though I cherish the values of compassion and solidarity on which I was raised I am not nostalgic for the Soviet Union. But someone who does not make an attempt to comprehend Russia as it was then, in the hard years after 1991, will, I think, struggle to understand much about Russia as it is now.

The following chapters do not constitute a classic autobiography, in which the account begins in the cradle and carries on in exhaustive detail up to the present day. Instead they are made up of a number of key episodes in my life, which I will expand to allow me to reflect on the wider context in which they occurred, so that Russia's story runs in parallel to my own. It will be arranged in the form of flashbacks, each prompted by a dramatic or meaningful moment during my time at Russian Railways, which will allow me to roam freely across Russia's vast geography, to examine its history and to introduce many of the book's major themes.

But before I go any further, I want to explain why the railways occupy such a unique place in our consciousness; and also to try and give a sense of how looking at its railway system might help you understand something of the way in which my country's magnitude has conspired with its history to present Russia with a unique set of complexities, challenges and contradictions, which demand in turn an equally particular brand of response. It is one thing, I have learned, to look at maps or pictures, it is another thing entirely to see at first hand the conditions and characteristics that make Russia like no other nation on the planet.

There was one thing that many of the hundreds of thousands of those Soviet citizens who were condemned to those gulags situated in Siberia's remotest corners did not realise when they first arrived. The tangled skeins of barbed wire that surrounded the camps were not the main barriers to escape. These barriers could, with a certain amount of ingenuity and determination, be penetrated. What really stood between the inmates and freedom was geography.

They were surrounded by a wilderness so vast that escape was almost impossible: countless miles of inhospitable terrain lay between their new quarters and the nearest settlement; they were almost as lonely and isolated as it is possible for a human being to be. The sheer size of Russia was sufficient to keep them captive.

• • •

If you settled into an aeroplane in London and flew for ten hours you would be able to step off in the United States, India, perhaps even China. Countries on the other side of the world. But if you were to take a ten-hour flight from Moscow, the chances are you would land somewhere like Vladivostok – many miles away, and yet still part of the same country. Today the Russian Federation covers over a ninth of the world's land surface and spans eleven time zones. Its population of 146 million includes some 200 discrete ethnic groups who between them speak over 100 languages. They live, variously, in cities and steppe, in arctic and sub-tropical temperatures, but they are all connected by the railways, which have played an enormous role in the process of enabling the heterogeneous people of Russia to cohere into a single, unified, state.

Before the railways came, it used to take as long as half a year to send messages from St Petersburg to the outlying regions; disputes were often settled by the governors of those areas bordering China well before their instructions from the Tsar ever arrived. The steel tracks that began to spread across the country's vast expanses completely changed the way people lived. Indeed, they are still changing people's lives today – given that most cross-country flights within Russia remain relatively expensive, railways will always be a primary means of traversing it.

You could almost say that the railway system is the lifeblood of the country: it keeps people and essential goods moving and enriches every organ it touches. For a long time it was also one of the most effective ways of conveying information. There's a story that in 1917 the only way people in far-flung regions in Russia

9

found out that the tsar had been overthrown and that in his place a new Bolshevik regime had come to power was because the trains had a different emblem on the front.

I have read before that spiders use their webs as an extension of their brains. One might say the same of Russia and its railways. It is through our railways – and the ingenuity, bravery, skill and vision displayed by the men and women who have worked on them – that we have come to know our countrymen; they are the stitches that hold this dizzyingly vast patchwork of people and territories together.

Until you have seen its seemingly endless vistas – the tundra blanketed by six feet of winter snowfall, the swamps drowned under water deep enough to swallow a man without trace, the almost hallucinatory monotony of the birch-tree forests that line mile after mile after mile of track – pass in a blur by your carriage, you cannot begin to comprehend the overwhelming immensity of the country, or the brute-scale problems this inevitably brings in its wake. Some of these are simply a question of logistics; others are the result of the complex interplay between the landscape and the infrastructure laid atop it.

Imagine, for example, that you are contemplating organising a train to run between Moscow and Vladivostok, a journey that lasts nearly a week. The locomotive's driver obviously cannot pilot the train for seven days without rest, so at eleven-hour intervals you have to make available some means to ensure they can be relieved.

If you were in Britain, it is likely that the rail company could simply send a taxi to pick the driver up and take them to the nearest motel. But while you do not tend to find motels, or even anything resembling them, in the middle of Siberia, your employees still need to rest and relax; perhaps most importantly, they need to eat.

So you establish special rest houses for the locomotive brigade – complete with saunas, cinemas and canteens. Then you need to start thinking about other things. At each of the rest houses someone will be tasked with checking the drivers' mental and physical health before they begin work – they cannot be allowed to control a train if they are tired, or sick, or drunk.

And of course, it is not only the driver who needs looking after. There are no workshops capable of locomotive maintenance a hundred miles into the Siberian forest, or anywhere with a tank of sufficient capacity to contain the amounts of gas and diesel the train consumes, so, again, it is the railway system that must provide them.

Once you have built all of these facilities, you have to populate them. Which presents new challenges. Who will look after children while their parents are at work? Special kindergartens and board schools where the kids can be cared for and educated have to be established. Before you know it, you realise that the railways are responsible for supporting a hugely complex network of people and services, in which every element is closely linked; it is almost like an ecosystem: if you remove one link in the chain, then the whole structure risks falling to pieces (which is one of the reasons why every metre of railway infrastructure must be watched and maintained constantly).

You realise too that each solution presents a new problem of its own. You need to provide hospitals for the workers along the route (because none exist in the area already; Russia's first comprehensive healthcare system, outside of the armed forces, was created by the railways), but then the hospital needs to be staffed and maintained, the doctors and nurses must be housed … the logical consequence of this is that there are a number of towns in Siberia that owe almost every aspect of their existence to the railways. (One of the great privileges I enjoyed as president of Russian Railways was the opportunity to look through the blueprints for the original Trans-Siberian route. Seeing how the architects of this great Russian endeavour had mapped out a new kind of life for every small town along the route, one complete with schools and hospitals, was an extraordinary experience. In an era when only a tiny proportion of the country was literate, and an even smaller percentage of the population had access to any kind of healthcare provision, it was an amazing, unprecedented investment in a better future. And, again, it is a tradition that persists. Even today, in some of the more far-flung areas of Russia you would struggle to find any doctor working outside of a railway hospital.)

You also have to quickly become accustomed to working in circumstances that would be unimaginable for most other Europeans. I remember a visit from the Italian Minister of Economic Development, Federica Guidi, whose brief included investment in her country's railway system. When she arrived, we were experiencing temperatures of around -25 degrees (she was dangerously underdressed, a situation we immediately resolved by swaddling her in thick furs). As we walked around, a member of the delegation asked my people the same question three times, but even when a translator was summoned our workers could not understand what she was asking. The Italian had wanted to find out how long the severe weather would prevent Russian Railways from operating, an enquiry that had prompted two distinct types of bafflement: firstly, in a country where temperatures often fall below -50, what we were experiencing was not severe; and secondly, it was inconceivable to us that they should ever stop us going about our business. The most we would ever consider doing would be to reduce the number of carriages and the weight of the train (because in freezing conditions metal becomes brittle, to the point that it shatters if struck with a hammer) or cut the speed. Stopping the service is not an option.

And yet, of course, in addition to the problems that you can anticipate, you also have to find a way to accommodate the kind of unruly event that tumbles out of the sky and upsets all of your careful plans. A moose might wander onto the line (there is no feasible way of fencing in every segment of our 85,000km of track) or the driver might suffer a sudden attack of mental illness (in one terrifying incident, in which a disaster was only narrowly averted, a driver came to believe that God had instructed him to smash his locomotive into the next train he saw – luckily the signals we began to receive warned us so that we could turn the electricity in that sector off).

All this is, I suppose, a way of arguing that Russia's railway system is as good a metaphor for the country as a whole as any other. The product of a very particular set of historical circumstances, it is at once almost inconceivably huge and head-spinningly complex, and cannot be reduced to a simple, monolithic entity. Contained in its vastness is an array of interlinking parts trying to function as a cohesive whole in the face of circumstances (some that can be predicted, some that emerge completely unannounced) so extreme that they inevitably exert a profound and distorting influence on any attempt to operate within them.

However, although the symptoms of this situation may sometimes appear bizarre, or incomprehensible, the causes, if you look carefully enough, are often more straightforward. Sometimes all that is needed to provide you with a different perspective is for someone else to turn the looking glass a couple of degrees in another direction. I cannot pretend that this book will provide you with all the answers about contemporary Russia, but I hope that it will leave you in a position to ask the right questions.

CHAPTER TWO

SMILE! YOU'RE
IN THE USA

Language is not just about grammar or vocabulary: a single sentence is the reflection of centuries of mentality and traditions; it encodes the differences between cultures.[1] Two people from different countries might be able to understand each other's conversation, but there will still be a gulf of comprehension between the native speaker and his interlocutor. Sometimes this

---

[1] In 2008 I was given a stark reminder of the way in which an entire language can come to bear the weight of history on its shoulders. It was a time when we had been doing a great deal of work with Siemens. But one thing puzzled me: I remember asking their CEO Peter Löscher why it was that during meetings Chancellor Angela Merkel, who had been born in East Germany and was known to speak fluent Russian, confined herself to communicating through a translator. My policy has always been: if I know one word in Chinese, I will use it; if I know three words in German, I will use them. Why would you not? I could not understand why someone who knew Russian as well as her should not employ it when she was in Russia – it was as if she were in the grip of some kind of phobia.

Two weeks later a friend of mine sent me a letter saying that the chancellor wanted to meet me in Berlin. She greeted me at the door of her office's antechamber, and immediately began to talk to me in Russian. 'She said, Mr Yakunin, you're right, I do have a phobia about speaking in Russian. When I was a young girl my bicycle was stolen by a Soviet soldier and ever since then I have felt what I suppose is animosity towards Russians.' 'Mrs Merkel,' I replied immediately, 'There is a large department store around the corner. If I thought for one second that it would heal your wound, I would rush across and buy every single bicycle they have, but I'm not sure it would help.'

can be a question of jokes or anecdotes that get missed; at other times it is about the manner in which the words are delivered.

Russians have a gift for concision and compression in their speech that I have seen other cultures take for bad manners. We like to cut corners in conversation sometimes, so we can get to our point more quickly, but this brevity – boom, boom, boom, boom – can sometimes leave foreigners with hurt feelings (which is precisely the opposite of what we want to achieve: the Russian mentality aims at making friends). I have been told that even our body language has the potential to send out an unwontedly aggressive message.

There's a traditional Russian story that sums this up – sometimes an anecdote can explain as much about a culture as whole books full of sociological analysis. One day a landlord visits his premises. As he and his manager walk around the land they come to a small stream that divides two fields. Anxious not to spoil his boots unnecessarily, the landlord very politely says to his manager: 'Ivan, it would be good if you could build a small bridge here.' The manager agrees. Two months later the landlord returns and is surprised to find that his manager has not built the bridge. They talk again. 'Listen,' the landlord says, 'Ivan, please could you build a bridge so I don't get my feet wet.' 'Of course,' comes the reply. The next time the landlord descends on his property he sees to his distress that the bridge still has not been built. Unable to control himself he hits the manager and exclaims, 'Bloody hound! Just do what I ask!' The manager stands up, turns to his boss with an innocent look on his face, and says, 'Sir, why didn't you tell me what to do from the beginning? Now I understand!'

I remember that when Russian Railways was building the

high-speed Sapsan line between Moscow and St Petersburg, we had entered into a partnership with the German company, Siemens. But to begin with we had problems like you would not believe, with neither side able to find a way of communicating happily with each other. The Germans complained that the Russians were rude, inefficient and understood nothing. The Russians, by contrast, perceived their counterparts as indolent and unwilling to adapt themselves to the local ways of working. Unable to see an immediate solution to the impasse I called Peter Löscher, who was then president of Siemens, and with whom at the time I was only scantly familiar. I told him about the problems in hand and we both agreed that a great deal was at stake: it was Russian Railways' very first international agreement.

We decided that Löscher's chief engineer would fly out to Russia, where, along with those of his employees who were already on the ground, they would attend a meeting conducted in the time-honoured straightforward Russian Railways style. They watched as we got going, everyone present putting their views across forcefully, and at the end I turned to the room and said,

> Listen, I don't give a damn if you are Russian or German, we have
> a mutual target and you are responsible for the work. The image
> of both companies is on the line here, and if you don't deliver, it
> doesn't matter to me where you come from, I'll eat you alive. And,
> by the way, Mr Löscher knows about this meeting.

Finished. With that I left the room, leaving the men and women assembled there to absorb the message I had just delivered. My speech had been very short, very precise. I barely did anything to adorn it – I did not raise my voice, and I stripped my face of any signs of emotion – but it must have worked. Two days went by, and after that we never saw another problem. And still, years on, whenever I see Mr Löscher and his chief engineer, they remind me of it, making friendly jokes about what they witnessed. I think it has stayed with them because my approach was so different to what they were used to in boardrooms in the West. American-style companies smile as they're stabbing you in the back. You never have a hint of impending danger; at least not until the next day when you receive an envelope containing your severance package. (Of course, in Russia we are as capable of being as surprised by the mores of other nations as they are by ours. Drinking at lunch during a working day is, for us, uncon-scionable, which is some distance from the French perspective on this. I remember being called by a bewildered engineer who, on a trip to France, had been offered wine at 1 p.m. Anxious though he was of causing offence, he was also completely un-accustomed to the idea of having alcohol so early in the day. Being able to work effectively with people from other countries demands a very particular skillset.)

Not all of my experiences of the ways that different civilisa-tions interact with each other ended as neatly as the Siemens episode. My spell in New York City during the '80s – a location so distant and strange that my mother later told me that when I departed, to her I might as well have been heading for the moon – was a case in point. But it would provide me with my first encounter with a role I have come increasingly to inhabit as my career has progressed – that of a bridge between two groups who cannot and will not understand each other.

My family arrived in the United States in 1985 and returned to St Petersburg in 1991. Our time in North America coincided almost exactly with the Soviet Union's Gorbachev-inspired era of perestroika and glasnost. The broken country we had moved back to was almost unrecognisable from the superpower we had left six years earlier.

Though that is not to say we hadn't been able to tell that there were cracks in the USSR's edifice. By the end of the 1970s, there was a growing sense that something was going wrong. People did not go out onto the street to demand change; nobody, with the exception of a few scattered groups of dissidents, was screaming or waving placards (perhaps we would have done well to remember that sometimes it is enough if even a small portion of the apple is rotten – before long the whole fruit will be spoilt). But, when our front doors were shut and we knew we were among friends, we discussed the setbacks of the system. No matter what we were told by the Politburo, or read in the pages of *Pravda*, we knew that living standards were falling – people in the provinces could go for years without seeing fresh meat – and it was manifestly obvious that the nation was no longer able to meet the economic targets it had set itself. Perhaps, we began to wonder, it never had. Then rumours began to circulate. Some were fairly benign – nobody was too bothered by the allegedly gilded lives led by those who were known as the 'Golden Kids', the children of party bosses. And there was nothing that new or surprising about the dark mutterings regarding links between the CPSU (Communist Party of the Soviet Union) hierarchy and men involved in illicit forms of entrepreneurship. But we were electrified by whispers, which began tentatively before steadily becoming more insistent, about the use of force in Novocher-kassk twenty years beforehand to suppress a protest by workers there. We tried to stitch the whispers we heard, the little shreds of information, into something we could understand. Though everything had been hushed-up by the authorities, little by little it grew apparent that there had been a demonstration there in 1962 and that the military had fired on the protestors, killing many. What kind of state did this to its own people?

We watched streams of men coming back from Afghanistan – still believing them to be hero veterans – the body bags hidden from public view; we watched our government on television, grey decrepit men stiffly reading pre-prepared statements that told us nothing, that *meant* nothing. Leonid Brezhnev presided over years of stagnation, Yuri Andropov was clever and resource-ful, but only rose to the top once he was already critically ill, and then there was Konstantin Chernenko, who crept into view, blinked for a moment, then crept off stage to quietly die.

But what you need to understand is that there was nothing inevitable about what occurred next, under Gorbachev. It is too easy to look through the wrong end of the telescope and assume that just because something happened, then it *had* to happen. You can find all the things that contributed to an event and call them symptoms, and before you know it you have what looks like a scientific thesis – but this is a dangerous game.

The Chinese have shown that it is possible to navigate the complex and challenging path that leads from a monolithic socialist state to something that at least has the appearance of a market economy. Of course, counter-factual history is an inherently treacherous business, but if you consider how much more advanced the Soviet Union was in comparison to China at the time, it is hard not to regret that this was a path we never travelled down. (Perhaps we would be living in a different kind of world today if the gifted Kazakhstani politician Nursultan Nazarbayev, an extraordinary, shrewd, cultured personality, who eschewed the nationalism that infected many of his contemporaries, had agreed to become the Soviet Union's Prime Minister when he was asked in 1991. His refusal marks another fork in the road of history.)

The vast majority of the USSR's citizens, including myself, still believed that the Soviet system should be modified, even quite substantially, but we did not want to see the whole edifice dismantled. And it would be a mistake to assume that the party itself was blind to the urgent need for change. In 1978, while I was still a young officer, I attended a special lecture delivered to a group of senior KGB officers and intelligence staff by a representative of the regional CPSU's headquarters. It expressed ideas that no dissident would have been brave enough to articulate at the time. We were told that if the CPSU did not take serious steps towards the reform of the social and economic structure of the Soviet Union in the next ten years, we would face a systemic crisis. (A lot of people do not know that the privatisations enacted in the '90s were inspired by theories originated in a research institute established by the then head of the KGB, Andropov, and members of the CPSU Politburo a decade earlier, to map out how to reform the Soviet system. The liberal reformers who came to prominence in the '90s, men like Anatoly Chubais, were just fledglings who came from a nest created by Andropov.)

Outside those privileged circles I witnessed a lot of criticism concerning the way in which our society was run, and yet I never was exposed to a purely anti-Soviet attitude. Of course, being young and sceptical we could not help but be perturbed by some of what we heard about the party elite. Most of the senior apparatus remained ideologically persistent Communists, and in theory their capacity for corruption was curtailed by the unofficial rule that meant they couldn't earn a salary in excess of that of a highly trained worker. Nor were they permitted to hold valuable private assets. But they occupied completely different houses, lived in separate villages, and obtained their clothes and food from special department stores (sailors, who had the access to foreign currency denied to the rest of the population, enjoyed this same privilege, but almost nobody else did). It was no wonder that Andropov was once moved to confess that the party leadership was running a country that it barely understood. These men spent their lives urging others to give more, to work harder, but they never took responsibility on their own shoulders; I do not think they ever truly understood the burden they were placing on the people's shoulders.

So we were sick and tired of the elderly leaders who we felt were not entitled to the huge power they wielded. The majority of the population remained supportive of the ideas of socialism and brotherhood with which we had grown up, but we also appreciated the necessity of reform; we wanted to change the crippled management system. This meant that paradoxically the jokes and tales we heard that reflected the weakness and inability of the old men who ruled the USSR – for example that Brezhnev mistook the Japanese ambassador for his Chinese counterpart and spoke to him for four hours without realising – were a kind of reassurance: we could persuade ourselves that as soon as we had new leaders, all would be well again.

And then came Gorbachev. He was the first senior figure in Russia I'd ever seen who could talk for hours to the people without stopping to refer to a script. When he said something it was as if he was taking the thoughts out of your own head; he appeared in public with his wife (which would have been anathema to his retiring predecessors); everything about him seemed unprecedented and fresh. I would later come to understand that he only masqueraded as a symbol of hope, but at the time millions of people were willing to follow him, as though he was the Pied Piper.

Though he was well educated in comparison to his comrades in the Politburo, they did not know that he was illiterate in terms of state governance, and naïve to the point of imbecility in his relations with the United States and its allies. They did not know that he had no idea what consequences would attend his reckless actions, which only had a thousand to one chance of success; that he would destroy the system he had set out to save, along with the lives of millions of ordinary people who existed within it. They did not know that he was unaware of his own limitations and of the gaps in his own knowledge, or that he had no intention of taking responsibility for any of this. (They did not realise, perhaps none of us did, that once a man was installed at the top of the system he attained something like papal infallibility, which meant that his capacity to effect monumental change, without checks or balances, was enormous; there was no one with authority to challenge the leader's wrong assumptions or ignorance. And even if we had, who could have suspected this young, benevolent-seeming man, who always said the right thing, of being capable of abusing this power?)

A tendency to indulge in wishful thinking is one of the most dangerous qualities a politician can possess. So perhaps it was Russia's tragedy that both Gorbachev and Boris Yeltsin were afflicted by it. I suspect Gorbachev was more of an idealist than the man who succeeded him, and I do not doubt that he wanted the best for the USSR. But his ideals were not accompanied by a practical scheme for implementing them. He did not want to break the Soviet Union apart, and yet once the process of disintegration had begun, he did little to stop it. Instead, he affected surprise at the consequences of changes he had himself set in motion, and seemed content to act as a spectator of his country's demise. Hundreds of thousands have died unnecessarily as a result, while 'Gorby' still poses as a great historical figure. (In 2016 he published a memoir, the Russian title of which translates as 'I remain an optimist', which reads like black humour to anyone who has spent time in the country his actions brought to its knees.) It might surprise you to read this, for I know he enjoys a hero's reputation in the West, but I am far from being the only person in Russia who sees the last leader of the Soviet Union in this way.

All this, though, was in the future. As far as the officials checking my documents at the US border were concerned, I had been posted to New York in 1985 to work as a diplomat – one of the Russian representatives on the United Nations' Committee on the Peaceful Uses of Outer Space. But I would be combining this with my work for the First Directorate of the Intelligence Division of the KGB, one of the most respected occupations in the Soviet Union. The education it offered you was on a par with anything you could find in Cambridge or Princeton; if you were ambitious, if you wanted to challenge yourself, you joined the KGB's foreign service, the First Directorate. But in those days, you did not apply for a position in the KGB; no matter how keen you were to join the organisation, you had to wait for them to contact you. It was considered somehow suspect to knock on their door and ask to be let in.

When a KGB officer first contacted me, I was aware of their prestige, but at the same time, there were certain elements of the security service's history that made me feel uncomfortable. My father-in-law came from what you might call the intelligentsia, and when he learned that I was contemplating signing up he was greatly concerned. We talked and he told me that of course it was for me to decide, but that there was one thing I had to remember. He told me:

> Our generation, we are the children of the frightened generation, for whom the night was a nightmare. Every evening, once darkness fell across the city, our parents would all lie gripped by terror, listening out for the growl of a car pulling up outside their apartment, which they knew would be followed by the crunch of boots on the staircase, and, finally, a knock at their door. The situation is different now, but that fear still lives on inside me.

I remember that I was so anxious about the prospect of joining and all that it entailed that for the first time in my life I learned where exactly my heart was located. I had been sitting in a Komsomol[2]

---

2 All-Union Leninist Young Communist League, a youth organisation dedicated to beginning the process of creating model Soviet citizens. It operated, to employ a sporting analogy, almost like a feeder club for the main CPSU. Membership was considered highly desirable and the sons and daughters of people such as priests were barred from joining.

leadership development class, when I felt a searing pain lance through my chest. I was rushed to hospital and after a series of checks I was informed that the pain was a response to the huge anxiety and tension swirling around inside me at the prospect of making such a momentous decision.

Not long afterwards, a family contact who was head of the Leningrad station's counter-intelligence branch summoned me to his office, where he talked to me for a while. He asked me questions about who I was, where I worked, then he thought for a while before turning to me and saying,

> Yakunin, why do you want to join our organisation? You are study-
> ing at a top research institute, you're about to get a PhD, there
> is a clear path ahead of you; why put all this at risk? Why join
> an organisation full of tension, danger, hard labour and possibly
> blood? It is a bloody heavy business, and, personally speaking, I
> don't think it is for you. Let somebody else do the dirty work.

What he was saying, in essence, was that I must be prepared to sacrifice everything I loved for the sake of my country, but then this was exactly what I had been brought up to believe. Service to the country and its people were the central elements of the ideological education I had received. I felt that the harder the work promised to be, the greater the contribution I could make to the nation I loved. I knew it would be challenging, and that I would be joining an institution with a complex, charged history, but what might have sounded to others like a warning was to me an incredible and exciting opportunity to help protect the ideals and nation that I cherished so dearly.

At the Dzerzhinsky Higher School and then the Andropov Krasnoznamenny Institute in Moscow, the KGB university for prospective intelligence officers, I learned a lot, perhaps more than I ever thought possible. I learned to speak English so well that I even began to think in the language. I learned about the panoply of techniques I would need to perform my role to the highest standards possible, skills that in the years that followed saved my life more than once. I also learned about the organisation itself. Far from being an omnipotent beast extending its tentacles across the world, the security services were subject to constant surveillance and guidance from the Communist Party. Even during the darkest days of Stalin's terror, I discovered, the decisions were not being made by the heads of the OGPU or the NKVD,[3] but by the so-called 'Troikas',[4] which were headed by regional party bosses. The Troikas had ceased to operate by the '50s, but the secret services remained subordinate to the party until the end of the Soviet Union. Decades later when I began my KGB training, almost the first thing we were told was that we were the armed instrument of the party. They gave the orders; our job was to follow them.

Along with the other new recruits, I was also taught about the values at the KGB's heart. There was much you might expect – about ideology, security and secrecy – but other aspects were more of a surprise. It was made clear to us that the recruits themselves were considered to be the organisation's most valuable

---

3 The OGPU and NKVD were two of the forerunners of the KGB.
4 Three-man-strong commissions who in the Soviet Union were employed as instruments of extra-judicial punishment. They were permitted to effectively bypass much of the existing legal apparatus – including the defendant's right to a full trial, legal aid or the presumption of innocence – in order to secure quick convictions.

assets. I discovered the truth of this early on in my career when I was struck down by a very severe trauma in my back.

It got so bad that I spent more than four months in hospital. Even after I had been discharged, I could not put on my socks or my underwear without my wife helping. My doctor recommended that in order to overcome the consequences of the injury I should follow a programme of complete rest, followed by a six-month-long course of physiotherapy, water treatment and rehabilitation. It was beginning to look as if my time in the KGB would be over almost before it had begun. It got so bad that I had already started to draft my letter of retirement. As a final resort, I approached the head of my department, a man reputed to be one of the toughest in the entire system – a merciless product of the previous era, so granite-hard that some people said you would struggle to find anything human in him. Almost before I'd finished outlining my problem, he had picked up the telephone, called my immediate superior, and said, 'Listen, from now until the end of this year, Yakunin is working only on my orders. You won't bother yourself about his timetable, you won't take any interest in his results; for one year he is my man.' He put down the phone and told me I was to carry on my treatment. I will be grateful to him for the rest of my life.

But these benefits were accompanied by responsibilities. We were not just expected to be steadfast and discreet in our work, it was made clear to us that, as part of the organisation's code of behaviour, we were never supposed to ask what kind of salary we might receive for fulfilling a particular role. Nor was it expected that we would try and negotiate any other kind of advantage. When I graduated from the Andropov Krasnoznamenny

Institute, I learned the truth of this for myself. It was considered likely that I would be posted to an English-speaking African country where the white residents lived like kings, but I asked if they had schools where my kids could study. It was a calculated risk: I knew I was considered one of the most promising cadets, so thought perhaps that I had more leeway than my contemporaries, and the idea of leaving my family behind for such a long time was utterly inimical to me. But it almost ruined my career. I was told that my request had been completely contrary to the tradition and rules of the service and it was immediately decided I would not be allowed abroad. I would have to wait four years until the general who had stated categorically that 'Yakunin can never work in the field abroad' eventually changed his mind and sent me to the US.

We left for New York at a strange time in the relationship between the Soviet Union and the United States. Though on the one hand it seemed as if Gorbachev's rise to power might herald a new era in which the hostility between our two nations might finally ease, this in itself was not sufficient to disperse the tensions and bitterness that had built up steadily in the years since the end of the détente that had reigned under Brezhnev. A considerable amount of raw feeling lingered after events such as the American wars in Vietnam and Cambodia, the shooting down by Soviet planes of Korean Air Lines Flight 902 in 1978 and Flight 007 in 1983, the USSR's invasion of Afghanistan in 1979, the USA's invasion of Grenada in 1983, and the way in which our nations had taken it in turn to boycott each other's Olympic Games.

Initially though, our concerns were somewhat more prosaic.

As I came with my wife and two sons through the terminal in Canada, where we had a stopover en route (the tensions between our nations meant that it was impossible to take a direct flight), we realised we had no experience of how to proceed to make our connection to New York; we did not even know how and when our flight would be called. I remember sitting there, munching on a sandwich, waiting in vain to hear the announcement. It was only when my wife suggested I speak to an official that we realised the plane was about to leave – I don't think that airport has ever seen four Russians run as fast as we did when we sprinted to make sure we didn't miss our plane.

We were followed by 200 kilogrammes of household possessions and two decades' worth of assumptions about American life, many of which were soon proven wrong. Before we left for the posting I had engaged in a period of study so intensive that by the end of it I could have worked as one of the city's tour guides. But no matter how much preparation you undergo, it is still difficult to adapt when you are thrust headfirst into a different culture. (That said, I was some distance from being like the old revolutionary I read about who visited New York City and was so shocked by the amount of food she saw on sale that she started to cry, or the two Soviet delegates who after observing one overstuffed candy store demanded to be taken to another to satisfy themselves that the first they had seen had not been a trick.)

Small things seem bigger when you are in another country. One thing that always struck me was the huge gulf between the ways in which Russian and American children behaved. Their children were completely unreserved – they had absorbed their parents' unlimited way of communicating – whereas Soviet kids were far more solemn and self-possessed. When we went to the UN on the day after our arrival to take photos for our passes, the photographer could not believe what he was seeing: 'Listen, you Russians, why do you always have such gloomy faces. Smile! You're in the USA.' He told my youngest son, Viktor, to say 'cheese' in an attempt to get him to grin. It was funny to discover that Viktor had a wicked sense of humour: he replied with the Russian translation 'сыр', whose pronunciation ('syr') certainly does not involve smiling.

Something of the American spirit must have rubbed off on the Soviet diplomatic community in the States, for it was far more democratic than its equivalents in other postings. For instance, usually the first secretary does not mix socially with the third secretary, but in New York there was a great deal of trust between us. Perhaps it was something to do with our generation – people who were well educated and who already had some knowledge of foreign culture. For instance, seven years previously I had travelled to Malaga on my first ever assignment, having been in- serted into part of a delegation of scientists who were attending a conference on semiconductors. (How surprised I would have been then if you had told me the circumstances in which I would encounter semiconductors later in my life.)

Even a couple of years after Franco's death, Spain seemed grey and lifeless, as if it was yet to recover from the legacy of El Caudillo's baleful reign – it was a marked difference to the sense of release and excitement that ruled Russia's streets during the final stages of perestroika. I would think of this visit to Spain again many years later when my path crossed with that of Juan

Carlos I, who was then the country's king. In the course of the curious, circumscribed childhood the dictatorship had restricted him to, the young royal became friends with a boy who would go on to lead the train manufacturer Talgo. When, during the 2000s, I returned to Spain as part of a Russian Railways delegation, who had travelled there to discuss the possibility of wider collaboration between our two companies, I was invited to meet Juan Carlos. The Spanish king was, they told me, passionately interested in a positive outcome for the deal. We talked and I came away struck by his warmth, and also his unaffected, democratic demeanour. A little later in Moscow this impression was reinforced when I received a call on my mobile. To begin with, I could not make out who I was speaking to. 'Who is this?' I asked, mystified. 'It is me, your friend Juan Carlos,' replied the voice on the other end of the line.

I would have been surprised if, in the middle of the cold war, you had told me that I would later find myself on friendly terms with a Western monarch, but then I also own the original copy of the eighteenth-century declaration of friendship made between the tsar and the Spanish king – a document that highlights the fact that, far from being a peripheral nation with one foot in Asia, Russia has long been an integral part of Europe's economic and political history. (People are accustomed to seeing us as somehow 'other', but our culture has long been meshed with that of Western Europe. Consider, for instance, how large parts of Tolstoy's *War and Peace* were written in French. It was the product of a society in which it was taken for granted that anyone reading the novel would also be fluent in more than one language.) I took much pleasure from the idea of being another link in a several-hundred-years-long chain of amity and cooperation.

But back in 1985 I was in a *kap-strana* (the more colloquial iteration of *kapitalisticheskaya strana*), what we Soviets called a capitalist country, for only the second time in my life (admittedly twice more than nearly all of my comrades); and it was in New York that I noticed that while we had been taught to treat our personal interests as secondary to those of the state and community, in the Western mentality they were paramount. On my first trip on the subway, I offered to give my seat up for a very stout old black lady who had got on at the stop after me – I still remember the shocked faces of the other passengers, even the woman herself. A man in a suit and tie giving up his seat for an old black lady? It was as if there had been a small explosion; they looked at me as if I was a lion that had come from the moon. I understood I had done something unusual, and did not make the same mistake again. I always stood when I travelled on public transport after that.

Perhaps I should have been more assiduous in learning how to advance my own needs: the apartment we were first assigned, which was in the Bronx and in one of the city's cheapest high rises, was, now I look back on it, a disgrace, an embarrassment, evidence of a system that could be crudely indifferent to the feelings and comfort of its own people. We may have been considered valuable assets, but this was not always reflected in our salary, nor in the accommodation with which we were provided when we were posted abroad; any attempts to try to convert the prestige we enjoyed into material benefits, or increased personal comfort, were considered evidence of a suspect character. The carpet in our Spartan quarters was so thin and worn out as to be unusable, and instead of beds, my eldest son was expected to sleep on boxes that had once contained guns (God knows how they had got there), with boards resting on the top. It was puzzling to find ourselves placed in such conditions, but at the time I didn't pay it much attention; I did not understand that some diplomats were able to secure money from the representatives to the UN to buy new furniture and improve their flats. Nor did I realise to begin with that my salary – half of which was paid in dollars, with the other half deposited in roubles into my account in Russia – was lower than a garbage collector's at the New York Department of Sanitation.

In truth, the diminutive size of my salary never bothered me – it was enough for me and my family, so why should we have asked for more? – but I still feel lacerated by one memory in particular. Alexander Yakovlev, then the top ideologist of the CPSU and a close ally of Gorbachev, came to visit the United States at the very end of the 1980s. He was a man I had always respected; I even read the book he'd written about American politics before crossing the Atlantic. And then we met him. There he was, slouching in front of us in a gaudy tracksuit, which emphasised his huge belly. How could we take it as anything other than a calculated way of showing the contempt he felt for us? He made desultory conversation for a while, before producing an enormous shopping list of consumer goods – clothes, radios, tape recorders, jeans – that we were expected to provide for him out of the special fund that every KGB station retained for the use of visiting members of the Politburo. (We were not encouraged to ask questions about what they spent it on; indeed we were warned off making any kind of investigation into the lives of senior party officials.) This was the man who, like Gorbachev, had for years been telling us how we should be devoted to the party, devoted to the country, devoted to the ideas of socialism, and here he was, indulging in unabashed, hedonistic consumerism. I was not alone in feeling humiliated that for so long we had been fooled into thinking that Yakovlev actually believed in the sentiments he had expected us to embrace without question. It told me everything I needed to know about the kind of men who were now leading our nation.

This feeling was only reinforced later when I heard an interview with Yakovlev that was broadcast on the television. The man who, in 1991, brokered the meeting between Yeltsin and Gorbachev that sealed the fate of the USSR talked about how, in 1946, he had observed a group of former Soviet prisoners of war being shepherded into cattle trucks destined for the gulags of the Far East. He said that he could not comprehend how Red Army men whose only 'crime' was to have been captured by the Germans could be declared traitors by their own government. It was at that moment, he claimed, that he suddenly understood the rottenness of the socialist system. While I have always felt sympathetic to these unfortunate Soviet soldiers, and believe that the treatment they received on their return was terribly unfair, I cannot help feeling betrayed by him. For the next three decades, he was the top ideologist of the Soviet Union; we were taught only to serve – no personal interests, no excuses, only orders, targets and achievements – while he and the others at the top of the party were living in a completely different world.

In those years I spent in New York during the 1980s I was, officially at least, responsible for helping to prepare the positions of the Soviet Union on essential legal and technical issues, some of which had been under discussion for many decades. One of the most prominent of these was the question of geostationary orbit, which is crucial for the placement of vessels such as communication and weather satellites. Developing countries were very conscious that outer space had already become a limited resource, one that had hitherto been monopolised by the first world. Their great concern was that when the moment arrived when they were in a position to launch a satellite, there simply wouldn't be any room for it up beyond the heavens. It sounds strange, even counter-intuitive, but it took up many hours of our time. Another pressing problem regarded the regulation of the use of nuclear power in outer space. What was the appropriate, ethical, practical way of disposing of the ensuing waste?

Much of what I did was routine work in which my engineering background proved invaluable. It was sometimes difficult to find solutions in a situation where 159 nations, many of whom did not have access to the information they needed to construct an informed opinion, were nevertheless all trying to advance their interests. However, it was a fascinating insight into the mechanism of international relations as it operated under the UN umbrella, and also an exemplar of the way in which professionals from a huge range of nations, many of which were still locked into the cold war's tensions, could come together in a spirit of amity and build a profound and lasting consensus.

This sense of cheerful cooperation was not always evident within the 1,500-strong Soviet diplomatic contingent, which was prone to the usual quarrels and tensions experienced by such groups (exacerbated, I have no doubt, by the strange environment and the pressures and dislocations that always attend being away from home for long periods). But I remain on good terms with many of my former comrades. In the circumstances, it was easy to form close personal ties, which often led to us supporting each other, even (perhaps especially) in emergencies. While we were still all in New York, I learned that the little daughter of one of my colleagues had a chronic disease requiring expensive treatment, which he just could not afford. I remember to this day how bitter his sadness was when he shared the news of her affliction with me. Though the common practice in such cases was an immediate return home for the whole family, because I knew them all well and was, moreover, aware of how valuable the work of my colleague was, I decided to help him. I had already made some good friends among Americans by that time, some of whom were doctors. I discussed the case in detail with one of them, and I am still grateful to that doctor who immediately offered a treatment at his clinic, free of charge. The girl was treated, and my colleague was able to remain in post.

I was actually one of the few intelligence officers who took his diplomatic cover work seriously, but nevertheless my shadow-life absorbed as much of my time as my day-to-day existence. The difference between diplomats and intelligence operatives is largely one of methodology: while the diplomat uses open, legitimate channels and sources of information, an undercover agent uses more diverse routes. Their prime targets exist in the shadows, hidden from public view. I was surprised by the furore caused by the news that certain members of Trump's team had met with Sergey Kislyak, the former Russian ambassador to the United States, for surely that is exactly what a diplomat *should* be doing. What else is he there for?

When one arrives as a secret services agent in another country, one quickly enters into an unspoken arrangement with the other side – a prickly kind of modus vivendi. Our end of the bargain was that we had to ensure that we behaved in such a way that we never unnecessarily inconvenienced or endangered our American counterparts, or, worse still, humiliated them. So if you noticed you had a couple of men from the other side on your tail, you did not make any efforts to lose them … unless you had very good reason to do so. Otherwise you'd face very severe consequences – at the very least, you'd return to your car and find all your tyres punctured.

But even if there was a certain amount of respect between the two sides, I knew it would be fatal if that relationship evolved into something resembling friendship. They could be small things in themselves – birthday cards thrown through the car window of an American counterpart, or those occasions when agents would approach their tails in a café and inform them that they did not need to think about moving for at least an hour since the agent was going to lunch with his family. I completely prohibited this kind of communication, because I knew how amity could shade into compromise. Be polite, behave appropriately, but never cross the line.

In those circumstances, you develop an extreme sensitivity to the world around you. By the end of my stay in New York I could tell within a split-second whether a car was following me – something about it, some minuscule detail, always gave it away. You were so energised and concentrated all the time that you got into the habit of hoovering up every bit of information the environment around you could provide. If you had even the slightest feeling that something was awry, then you cancelled the mission immediately, and nobody would challenge you for doing so; our instincts were trusted.

This meant that you also gained the ability to read people as if they were a book. By closely observing the expression in their eyes, or the tiny gestures that they did not even realise they were making, you could discern the motives or plans they were trying to conceal. Sometimes your own life, or the safety of your colleagues, depended on your ability to deploy this level of intuition. The ability to read body language, to read all of the signs that other people communicate unconsciously, has been a great advantage in my subsequent career. And, conversely, I can use my demeanour almost like an instrument to help me persuade and manipulate. We were taught how to subtly change the expression of our eyes, the tightness of our skin, the cast of our jaws. At times I can be all soft and full of laughter, at others I can be like a beast, but I never lose control of my emotions.

Because our true identity was soon known to the FBI, as well as all the other Soviet citizens working in the Mission, it would not be precisely true to say that I led a double life (though to this day two profoundly different incarnations of my curriculum vitae exist, very few people have ever seen the unexpurgated version). But I learned early on that to survive for any length of time in intelligence it was crucial that you found a way to separate your professional and private identities. I became like an actor who slips out of his character the very same second that he steps off the stage.

The life of a field officer is one devoted to trying to detect the weaknesses in others – weaknesses they then have to exploit. This is true of every country's special services. Agents must learn quickly that any exceptional, or abnormal, feature in another person's personality is the foundation of every attempt to recruit them. A married man who cheats on his wife. A gambler up to his eyes in debt. A devoted father who discovers that his daughter is sick. They are always interested in the sorts of desires that people work all their lives to hide in the shadows. When they look at a man, it is because they want to know what his weakness is: money, women … men. (When we ourselves were first targeted for recruitment by the other side, we were scrutinised for traits in our characters that might be used by a hostile counter-intelligence organisation looking to expose us. Any exceptional feature – whether good or bad – in a candidate's personality was considered dangerous. Bright stars were generally not welcome in the KGB – if nothing else, there was a danger that you might think too much about the nature of some of the work you were expected to undertake. Loyalty and readiness to obey were considered the most desirable qualities.)

Those who exist in a world of manipulation and deception know that it requires an incredible effort to ensure that you do not yourself become infected by the cynicism and cunning involved. I realised one day, during the months before I was relocated to the United States, that I had lost the ability to look at women normally – I could only see them from a professional perspective, as people who I might be able to persuade to participate in an operation. It hit me with the force of a revelation.

A little later on I went home and started watching the news on television, but I do not think I had realised the extent to which my work in the secret services – which should have remained a discrete element in my life – had begun to seep into every aspect of my existence. I started to make remarks inspired by the world-view that I had absorbed unquestioningly from my teachers and colleagues. We had been stuffed full of ideology, like geese being fattened for foie gras, and for a long time I swallowed it whole. I was just getting into my stride when my wife Natalia inter-rupted me: 'Listen,' she said, 'I can see some changes in you, and I cannot say that I like these changes.' She did not need to say anything more. I realised I was in danger not only of losing the person I loved above all others, but also my identity, and that was the most effective inoculation I could have received. Ever since then I have divided my personal and professional lives, and in doing so I have preserved my human individuality from being swallowed up by my professional personality. Those who could not locate this balance did not last long. (I was also required to hide much from my wife: she could not know where I was going, or who I was with, or for how long I would be gone. I had thought it was a burden I carried alone; only later would I see that care and worry had eaten away at her. After six years in the United States, the woman who had departed looking like a model returned with her steadily accumulated anxieties etched onto her face.)

We had to deal with the usual diet of traitors and defectors, but the most awkward situation came when one of our under-cover officers was detained by the FBI. He possessed a diplomatic passport stating that he was an international servant of the

United Nations headquarters, but the Americans did not care about this. Without much ceremony he was thrown into jail, and shortly after the whole contretemps was resolved, if you can call it that, by the expulsion of around thirty Soviet diplomats from the United States. (The agent who was caught was bailed for $2 million and then left the country having agreed to plead the specially agreed formulation 'no contest' to the charges levelled against him. This was an arrangement that interested one of the small-time mafioso he met in jail, who wondered whether the Soviet Union might pay to spring them out too if he promised not to engage in any criminal activity once he had moved to the USSR. His plea was, of course, ignored.) Unsurprisingly, the heads of the Soviet station posted out there were first on the list, which meant that suddenly I became one of the highest-ranking agents on the ground. I had hitherto been just a regional officer, and nothing in my career had prepared me for this overnight elevation. More than anything, it was strange to observe how the people around me changed. I stayed the same, but I was surprised to find that I would never be treated the same way again.

I met a lot of interesting people, like Russian and American cosmonauts, and I learned huge amounts from my contacts with diplomats, businessmen and administrators from the mayor's office. Sometimes I was called upon to work as a translator for politicians (they asked me to attend a meeting between the security personnel of Gorbachev, Reagan and Bush, but somehow, despite the fact that neither side spoke the other's language, they managed to communicate perfectly happily after several shots of whiskey – I just sat idle with my American counterpart in the corner of the room) and visiting scientists (my success or otherwise here was entirely dependent on the extent to which I could understand the theories the figure in question was propounding – I had trained in rocket science, yet a lot of the more advanced equations zipped right over my head). But for me, New York was just a place; it was an office, never a home.

Sometimes it seemed as if we were in a kind of exile; though only 4,000 miles separated us from home, we might as well have been on Mars. We could not phone our families and had to rely instead on infrequent letters from them, which always arrived months after they had been posted. The people we loved back in the Soviet Union exercised incredible caution when contacting us; they knew we had little chance of being able to visit our homes, except in the case of an emergency, so they were wary of sending us anything that they thought might hit us hard emotionally. It was two months before Natalia discovered that her father had died.

Russian papers only arrived weeks after they were first published. So eager were we to receive information from our country that we swallowed any scraps we could get, like starving men scrabbling over a crust of bread. Depending on what we read or heard, we swung wildly between puzzlement, fascination, and, more rarely, exultation. What made the situation more complex was that American newspapers such as the *New York Times* presented a picture of almost complete ruin and chaos. It sometimes appeared as if they had swallowed Rupert Murdoch's thesis – that the best news is bad news – whole. Every time I opened the pages of the American press I was left terrified for the safety of my parents and sister.

But then if we spoke to Soviet diplomats who had just stepped off the plane from Moscow we were told how the turmoil was accompanied by profound enthusiasm. That there were meetings taking place across the length and breadth of the country attended not by dissidents but rather by positive people seeking new lives, seeking new possibilities. We learned about the impact of dramatic legislation, like the 1988 Law on Cooperatives, which marked the first time in six decades that enterprises could be set up independent of the state, and saw how the new freedoms that were extended to the population encouraged a new spirit of openness and optimism. Suddenly, politicians were speaking without reference to Lenin, ordinary people could air opinions in public that just months before they would have been afraid of whispering to even their closest friends, and the state's entire administrative apparatus had been convulsed by a series of electric shocks.

However, the virtuous attempt at de-centralisation resulted in a crisis of authority, as people who had previously been frightened into obedience began to exploit the new freedoms they had been extended, a process exacerbated by an abrupt, but devastating, economic crisis.

In time, we got used to reading in the US press what, in our eyes at least, amounted to propaganda. It was strange to be told by Americans that St Petersburg had become a militarised zone guarded by roaming gangs of cadets, or that out-of-control demonstrations were tearing the country apart. More often than not, one could laugh, but there was nothing funny about the atmosphere that still reigned even two years after Ronald Reagan's 'Evil Empire' speech'. I returned to our apartment the following day to find my eldest son – who played baseball and collected *Star*

Wars figures; how different was he really to the American kids living all around him? – bewildered to think that people might hate him simply because he was Russian.

I remember too, how when a friend of mine tried to invite my kids to visit his own children's school at Red Bank in New Jersey, I had to tell him that I was terribly sorry, but that Soviet diplomats were prohibited from entering the borough because it was considered to be too close to a number of sensitive government installations, and that the prohibition extended to their families too. He looked at me with a mixture of scepticism and surprise. 'Your propaganda has left you silly; they are kids, of course they can come!' I had to tell him that they had the same diplomatic status as myself, and that I really did not think they would be given permission for this trip. 'Don't worry, I'm friends with two senators,' he said, 'I'll get this fixed.' Two weeks later I saw him again, he looked diffident, almost ashamed, as he turned to me and said, 'Listen, Vladimir, I never thought that in the United States the authorities could behave like that about two boys who just happen to be the sons of a Soviet diplomat.'

But our friendship survived this, and we remain close to this day. The force of his country's aggressive official position towards the Soviet Union paled in comparison to the warmth shown to us every day by men and women on the street. They showed that they were above ideology and dogma, and that what mattered to them was forging friendly relations with other humans, no matter who they were, or where they were from. We never saw any signs of hatred from the country's ordinary citizens. On the day that I found my son so upset by the knowledge that he was a member of a so-called Evil Empire, I came to understand how deeply shocked he really was. So I rushed to the women of the UN's hospitality committee, who assured me that they were horrified by their president's words, and immediately arranged for my son to get tickets for the Christmas party at Macy's department store. For us, this felt as prestigious and exciting as the New Year's Eve party for children that was held every year at the Kremlin. We were met at the door by the women from the hospitality committee, who immediately involved my son in every game going. They were so unbelievably warm and kind that for the first time since we had moved to New York he started to speak in English.

On another occasion, on a trip to a remote lake to take my sons fishing, I accidentally locked my keys in my car. We were in the middle of nowhere, and to this day I still have no idea what I would have done if a police car had not drawn up beside us. The officers got out of their vehicle and asked whether we needed any help. 'Yes,' I said, explaining the situation. 'It seems I do.'

They presented me with two options. The first involved using their guns to shoot the door open. It would have undeniably been effective, but the car was a brand-new Buick and I did not fancy explaining to the Soviet Mission what had happened to their new investment. OK, they said, here's the second option: there's an individual who has just been released from one of our cells who is something of an expert at getting into locked cars, we can probably persuade him to lend a hand.

So we went back to the station where they immediately ordered an enormous pizza to keep the boys happy. I was feeling somewhat discombobulated – it is a strange experience for a senior Russian diplomat to spend any time in an American police station, whatever the reason – but those guys treated me as if they had known me all their lives. After forty minutes, they came to me and said, 'Mr Yakunin, you can go to your car now,' and there it was, the door open, the keys exactly where I had left them. There was no sense that they saw us as members of the Evil Empire, no sense at all that they saw us as anything other than a regular family who needed help.

We may talk differently, we may hold our cigarettes in a completely different way, but at the end of the day we are all human. People are people. We all want to live in peace, to have a good job and a nice home, for our family to be happy and our kids to get a good education. And never was this spirit more in evidence than in the response I witnessed to the catastrophic Spitak earthquake in what was then the Soviet Republic of Armenia.

The Soviet community in New York woke up on the morning of 7 December 1988 to be greeted by horrific news of death and destruction. The town of Spitak had been completely destroyed by two devastating shocks that struck just minutes apart. In fact the damage to its infrastructure and high-rise buildings was so severe that it could not be rebuilt – a completely new settlement had to be created on top of the wreckage. The nearby city of Leninakan (renamed Gyumri after the collapse of the Soviet Union), the second largest in the country, saw 80 per cent of its buildings turned into ruins. Over 25,000 lost their lives, and twenty times that number were left homeless. There were extreme shortages of clothing, blankets, excavators and medical equipment for procedures such as dialysis and blood-transfusions. The situation was so serious that, for the first time since the Great Patriotic War[5] (when the Allies proved that international cooperation between

5 The name by which the Second World War is known in Russia.

47

theoretically opposed power blocks was achievable, and replete with possibilities for mutual benefit), the Soviet Union appealed for help from the outside world. The nation's representatives in the United States, like its diplomats in dozens of countries across the globe, were told to put everything they were doing on hold, and to do everything within their power to assist the relief effort.

Nobody cared what job you did. You were freed of all responsibilities in order to enable you to gather assistance and support for the beleaguered victims of this natural disaster. For my part, I opened the Yellow Pages and found the address for the New Jersey headquarters of the Armenian General Benevolent Union. Without telephoning ahead, I arrived to find that their board meeting was in session. Once I had explained to the secretary who I was and why I was there, I was ushered into the room where, aware of the strength of my feelings, I spelled out the situation as calmly as I could. They immediately agreed to help, and would go on to do an enormous amount.

They collected clothes and blankets, and arranged an expedition by a special medical care group. Together, we located the best medical equipment we could find: everything from boxes of antibiotics from Pfizer to four special waterbeds for those suffering from bad burns, and several cars fully equipped to work in emergency areas. I remember how we went to the airport late at night, and how everyone there on the dark runway helped to create a chain to pass the packages containing the relief goods into the plane's cavernous hold. Even the airport staff were helping; in fact, the only men who stood aside, not lifting a finger, were the FBI agents who had shadowed my journey. They just watched, impassively, as if none of this was their concern.

Although the work itself was hot and heavy, we were outside in a New York winter and the temperatures outside had plummeted. Luckily I had two large bottles of vodka with me, so I asked the pilot if his crew had anything to eat and he produced a big pile of sandwiches, which we swallowed down with the spirits. Everyone shared except, of course, our friends from the American security services.

It was a huge job and at every turn I was struck by the Americans' ability to respond with unstinting generosity to a tragedy suffered by others thousands of miles away. It was then that, just before he climbed into the waiting plane, I heard a doctor called Vladimir Kvetan, who had left Czechoslovakia as a boy with his parents in 1968, saying to Richard McOmber, a representative of the Armenian General Benevolent Union who was married to an Armenian woman called Adrienne: 'Listen, I am going to the USSR to help people, but if I do not return in one week then you will know that I am in the hands of the KGB and you should do something to get me out.' How could I not respect his dignity and courage? How, indeed, could I not be struck by how ludicrous it was that I should consider him and many others like him, men and women who became lifelong friends, as enemies?

Three years later, I was saying goodbye to the American friends I had met during the crisis. 'Why go back to Russia during this period of turmoil?' Richard McOmber asked me. 'Russia will calm down after a year; everything will be OK and you can go back then.' I thought for a second before I replied. 'If this process has started in Russia,' I told him, 'then there's no way it will be over within a year. It will make no difference if I wait or not.' Unfortunately, I was right.

CHAPTER THREE

WHEN YOU COME TO ME TO ASK FOR SOMETHING, BRING ME SOMETHING IN RETURN

In 1992, inspired by my experiences and observations of successful entrepreneurship in New York – and specifically by the World Trade Center – I initiated the creation of an international business centre in St Petersburg. My colleagues and I believed that this was a new page in Russia's history (something that we would soon learn was an illusion), and that it was time, in the interests of better collaboration between Russia and the West, to help facilitate foreign investment into the country's economy.

With a kind of inevitability – a blackly humorous turn of events that seems to characterise my country – the building we secured the right to develop had previously been occupied by the local Communist Party, and although we had the lease for the entire property, it was decreed that one of our tenants should be the Russian Communist Workers' Party, a political organisation founded by hard-line Communists when the official Communist Party had been banned in November 1991. For a while, our work there seemed like a metaphor for some of the wider struggles occurring in the rest of the country. While we were trying to make the best of the opportunities offered in the new polity, trying to create something positive out of the ruins of a disintegrated system, Gennady Zyuganov's reconstituted Communist Party of the Russian Federation and their allies, who held the largest block of seats in the Duma, Russia's parliament, still seethed with resentment. They could not accept that times had changed, that the Soviet Union was no more. I, like many others, had mourned its demise, but I knew too that we would achieve nothing by trying to turn back the clock.

I remember that almost the first money that we, along with our partners from Israel, invested was used to renovate the toilets there – they were disgusting, horrible relics. Almost as soon as the work was completed, men from the RCWP broke in overnight; they took hammers to the toilets and mirrors. It was mad, irrational, but the country was disintegrating; it was just how things were. They were there for years, paying no rent, cranking out their increasingly eccentric propaganda. For a long time they insisted on flying their flag (which was indistinguishable from the Communist Party's old one) from the roof of the building. Each morning they would raise their standard, as if to prove they were still alive, that the battle against capitalism continued. They seemed to believe that, with this small ceremony, they could somehow conjure the regime of the hammer and sickle back from the dead.

In response we hired a cutter and a crane. The cutter was

supposed to remove the flagpole, but it was so firmly fixed into the roof and its structure that each time the workmen tried to dig it out it felt as if the entire building was jumping up. So we hired specialist equipment at great cost and finally managed to get rid of it. The next night, members of the RCWP penetrated the roof and erected a rickety homemade post from which they flew their flag. Once again they had proved they were alive, that they were still fighting the bloody capitalists. And perhaps they had a point; after all, they were not the only people who understood how seismic were the changes initiated by the disintegration of the old order.

When Vladimir Putin, speaking many years after the event, described the collapse of the Soviet Union as a geo-political catastrophe, he was murdered in the Western media. They treated him as if he was some kind of revanchist, desperate to restart the cold war and cover the country with gulags. But it was how we all felt; it was not an act of blind nostalgia to say this, just a pragmatic assessment of its profound political impact. The collapse of such a huge, complex system, with its enormous gravitational pull, created consequences of a scale that can only be comfortably compared to an earthquake, with shockwaves sent across the globe in its aftermath.

For decades there was a familiar balance of power in the world, underwritten by a nuclear deterrent, which to a large extent ensured stability in areas defined by histories that might as well have been written in blood. Look at what happened during the break-up of Yugoslavia, look at what is happening in Ukraine, think of the lopsided way in which the United States now exerts its force, almost unimpeded, in any country it wishes. The Soviet Union was an enormous presence, involved in ways large and small on every continent, and then over the course of a handful of months it withdrew completely, taking with it its money, men, weapons, scientists, teachers. How could this change not be experienced as a fundamental shift in the lives of billions of people?

I believe that in truth we have still not taken full measure of the consequences; as Zhou Enlai is supposed to have said about the after-effects of the French Revolution: 'It is too early to judge.' Many people who lived through this era will have their own stories about what they saw – these are mine.

My family returned to St Petersburg on 7 February 1991, in time to see the denouement of the catastrophe that Gorbachev had set in motion years earlier. It was a personal tragedy for me; my country was being dissolved. A whole way of life, extirpated. Everything I had been trained to do had been rendered meaningless by a few flicks of Gorbachev's pen. At that moment I did not care about history or global politics – I cared that my homeland was being wrecked. For my sons' generation it was harder still. The last years of the Soviet Union were perplexing and harsh for them; the story that they had been told about the world and the place they occupied in it was belied by what they actually saw with their own eyes. And yet communism was all the lost generation – as they soon came to be called – had ever known. Their fractured, dislocated experiences were summed up by a saying that proved immediately popular in St Petersburg: we were born in a city and country that no longer exist.

Our family went from a steady, predictable existence, where

we always knew when the next pay cheque was coming, and that the shops would always be full of food, to queuing anxiously for hours, hoping that there would still be a loaf of bread left on the shelves for which we could exchange the worthless coupons we had been given. We tried as hard as we could to recreate the normal existence we had enjoyed before, but it was rarely possible. If my son had a friend round for dinner, then Natalia would have to forgo her own meal to make sure there was enough to eat. For those who had lived through the starvation winters of '42 and '43, and who now saw food shortages and ration cards being issued again, it was as if the clock had been turned back fifty years.

When I was born, Russia was at the centre of the Soviet Union, one of the earth's two superpowers. I was a Soviet citizen, raised in Estonia, and all my life I had mixed freely with the USSR's different ethnicities, with Russians, Ukrainians, Armenians, Latvians and Georgians. We did not care what country our friend's father's father had been born in; we did not even notice.

Almost every element of my identity had been formed by experiences of existing, and participating, in the Soviet system. I sometimes think we were a little like fish in the ocean – we could not imagine how one might establish a different kind of life outside it. Along with my contemporaries, I had been brought up on the examples of the heroes of the Great Patriotic War and I still remember now how proud I was when, at the age of nine, I heard the news that the first Soviet Sputnik was launched. I was living with my grandparents at the time, and the entire population of their town of Nyandoma poured into the streets to celebrate (just as they did in settlements across the length and breadth of the nation). I had been an ardent member of the Komsomol and under its auspices had volunteered in the country's furthest corners. I had volunteered to build pipelines in Kazakhstan (the people there were strange and isolated; to them we might as well have been creatures brought back from space by Gagarin) and I also played my part in the *druzhina*, a kind of neighbourhood watch created by the Komsomol to make city streets safe by helping to clear them of their drunks, tramps and prostitutes – those people whom our society had deemed unde-sirable. As a diplomat, a scientist and intelligence officer I served my nation and my people loyally for decades. I knew its faults as well as anyone else: my closest friend now (I did not meet him until 1997) was prosecuted during the 1960s and at the age of eighteen was sent to Siberia for eight years. I had seen with my own eyes the subterfuges into which those who wished to adhere to even the most basic tenets of the Orthodox Church had been forced, and I had watched the tanks roll into Prague with the same moral queasiness as many thousands of others. But I also knew, and had benefited from, its many virtues. And yet now we were supposed to repudiate it, to abandon its precepts and move undauntedly into this disorienting new landscape.

In the early months of 1991, the state was completely unable to continue the way it had before. So many people – including my family – saw their savings obliterated by the collapse of the rouble and the complete disintegration of the country's financial system. Government enterprises, companies within the defence industry, they lost all of their orders overnight, and their em-ployees were left on their own. My brother- and sister-in-law were members of what was commonly referred to as the 'Soviet technical intelligentsia': well educated, cultured, with prestigious jobs at one of the leading defence industry research facilities. The family led a lifestyle that would have been the envy of millions across the country, with an apartment that had a separate room for their children, and even a private Lada car. But in the months after the collapse of the USSR, I saw their salaries cut so fiercely that it was as if they were not being paid at all. Their jobs became meaningless and their life savings evaporated. They lost their sense of direction and purpose overnight; they did not know what place they were supposed to occupy or what destination they should be working towards. What use were their skills now? Why continue to go into the office when there was no longer anything for them to do? What could the future offer them? There was no place for them in the new Russia. When I was a young man, they were probably the harshest critics of the 'Soviet way' I knew, but as the '90s drew on, it was little wonder that they began to develop a naïve nostalgia for the old regime, and a corresponding resentment for the new system that had replaced it, which evolved into a vicious suspicion of any attempts to reform the country.

Nobody had explained to them how they might go about building a new existence, and they were far from alone. St Petersburg was a city built on industry and research facilities, many of which had strong links to the military and navy. No other part of the country had as many inhabitants with university degrees or doctorates; it was the source of the vast majority of naval innovation, and a home for the brains behind the ill-fated Soviet space shuttle. And then suddenly this incredible accumulation of mental and technical resources was rendered worthless. A million people were effectively thrown onto the street with no means of fending for themselves. A further 500,000 simply left, while those who stayed were faced with a series of ugly choices. If you wanted to feed your family, could you afford to leave those valuable books to rest unprofitably on your shelves? If you wanted to clothe your children, could you justify holding your antique furniture back from the market round the corner? The people who knew how to work with their hands could always find something to do; if you had a practical skill then you could exchange your expertise for money, food or even a bottle of vodka. It was far harder to find anyone willing to swap a loaf of bread for a lecture on particle physics. For the doctors, scientists and teachers, tragedy, more often than not, arrived in cruelly measured portions of humiliation and stupefaction. We could barely believe it; the nation that had been the first to send a man into outer space could no longer even feed its own people.

Those who had become accustomed to the paternalism of the Soviet state – a secure job in a secure environment, free healthcare; in short a comprehensive safety net – now found themselves exposed. They were left only with feelings of unfairness and insecurity, feelings which still haunt them a quarter of a century later. Yet in some ways, these are the lucky ones. It has been estimated that 25 million people have died young since the collapse of communism. Some of them took their own lives – there were many macabre stories of entire families committing suicide together – while many others succumbed to illnesses, their bodies hollowed out by the strain of this new existence. Tuberculosis rates remained high at a time when it had almost been eradicated in the developed world, and countless men and women still struggle with chronic alcoholism. Even more serious for Russia's demographics after 1991 was that the birth rate plummeted; only in recent years, and with considerable state encouragement, is it beginning to pick up again. The life expectancy of Russian males fell from sixty-four in 1990 to fifty-eight in 1994.

In 1993, I discovered that even my own health was in tatters. My heart was hammering so hard in my chest that I could not lie down on my back; I had problem with my kidneys and my liver; it seemed that nearly every part of my body refused to function normally. I was still only forty-four, so this deterioration terrified me. At the hospital, I found out that the condition of my heart meant that I could not complete even half the exercises a man of my age might be expected to.

I was friends with a doctor at one of the hospitals in St Petersburg. He sat me down and explained this was not only the result of the huge tensions that had washed through my body over the past months, but also of a discrepancy between my mentality and the conditions out there in the real world. You have to change your attitude to life, he told me; you have to start to enjoy it, and stop allowing a feeling of responsibility to overwhelm you. If you continue like this, you will have only two years left – three, at best. Their prescription was as follows: each day I was to drink a glass of red wine and to make sure it was from a good vintage; I was also supposed to try and have as much sex as I could get, what we in Russia would call 'young hips without limit'. The first part of the advice was easy to follow, the second impossible for a man who had been born in Leningrad, not Sicily. I realised that I may have received the best education the Soviet Union could provide, and that I might be a highly trained intelligence officer used to danger and profound stress, but I was still made of flesh and blood, and that flesh and blood are ultimately vulnerable: they can only endure so much.

The citizens who had long been used to hypocrisy as a way of life – men like the old party bosses – simply changed their masks and embraced new opportunities to fatten their wallets. They did not suffer the same drastic changes to their existence as the regular people. More often than not they found ways of translating their influence and what was left of their principles into money. Those who had once upon a time fought hardest against vice opened the country's first X-rated cinemas; those who had warned us to be suspicious of Western influence began exploring how they could sell public utilities to foreign companies. Some members of the top brass were widely believed to be directly involved in selling weapons to the Chechen separatists their own troops were fighting.

Criminality surged, particularly murder and rape, and the police seemed unable, or unwilling, to do anything to stop it. Rather like the Wild West, the problem was not that people ignored or despised the law; the problem was that there were no laws. It was an ugly time. St Petersburg saw a spate of murders of people connected to its port. Auditors, port captains, directors of companies – all victims of the bloody vendettas of other men. I saw gangs of boys fighting in the street, observed by gangsters who watched from a distance, searching for new recruits – and begged my own son not to join them.

Petty infractions like theft and vandalism became an almost unremarkable presence in our lives. Boys who had once wanted to be doctors or engineers now openly boasted of their ambitions to become bandits, seduced by the sense of strength and power that haloed the gangsters who seemed intent on turning St Petersburg into their own playground. The social dirt that had been suppressed for eighty years rose to the surface and quickly infiltrated every corner of civil society. There was a wave of small-scale criminality – once, my own car was stolen while my driver had disappeared for five minutes to find a screwdriver. Ordinary Russian citizens, the men and women who had worked so hard in confounding, chaotic circumstances to try and keep their families alive, became completely disillusioned. Perhaps, in a world where one now often saw girls driven to standing on roadsides, hoping to be picked up by truck drivers, the old morals no longer existed.

Before 1991, it was the political system headed by the Communist Party and its repressive apparatus that had circumscribed the Russian people's freedom; now, it was a miserable compound of poverty and fear. If you cannot support your family or walk the streets safely, then your liberty has been stolen from you. Sometimes it was hard to believe that another, safer, city, a place where Westerners had marvelled at the way in which women could cross the city unmolested after dark, had once existed.

But some people thrived in this environment in which there were no longer any boundaries or restrictions. They rushed hungrily into new lives in which they started new enterprises – selling jeans and tie-dyed T-shirts – and looked forward to making their fortune. Thousands of businesses were started in the years and months that followed the end of communism; most failed, and yet a few survived and became successful. (The old-style bureaucrats who were clinging on to what status and power they had were as keen to make money as the younger generation who had made millions from buying state assets, but in most cases they were nowhere near as good at doing so.) It was a time when everyone was looking with big eyes for any opportunity to help support their families, a time when people could no longer afford to turn their noses up at prospects they might once have disdained.

Huge numbers of well-educated, well-trained men left their poorly paid police jobs to take up lucrative roles at security companies. There was no precedent for this in Russia, and it soon set off a dangerous spiral: the collapse of the state led to lawlessness, which in turn created a need for greater security, which could not be provided by a diminished police force whose impoverished officers had left to set up private security companies, a depletion that exacerbated the lawlessness. Inevitably, these shady, often semi-official, operations found that their work led them into contact with criminal organisations. While some businessmen chose to protect their operations by employing men who had previously worked in law enforcement, others looked to former criminals to play the same role. This contact could either lead to confrontation (which was usually accompanied by blood on the streets) or compromise (which would have been inconceivable to them in their previous careers). It all contributed to an insidious weakening of the rule of law. Business disputes were not settled in court; instead, this new breed of entrepreneurs sent their own private armies out to finish their arguments. The complex written and, even more importantly, unwritten rules that had previously governed society had been demolished, replaced by a single crude principle: when you come to me to ask for something, bring me something in return.

Boris Yeltsin looked like a man of the people – some joked that he even *smelled* like one – and he began his time in office as a dynamic advocate of the new freedoms offered us in the aftermath of the USSR's collapse. I think that he perhaps had his own version of what democracy should be like, and it would be difficult to argue that those around him were always committed to the purest forms of liberty, but he certainly helped protect our fragile democracy at a time when the nascent state seemed to be at its most vulnerable.

And yet while it is a great sadness that he is now remembered by many for his drunken foolery rather than his statesmanship, he was no more capable of imposing order on the country than his predecessor had been. Like Gorbachev, he made mistake after mistake and, like Gorbachev, it seemed that neither he nor the men around him were willing, or able, to learn any lessons. As his time in office dragged on, it became clear that events were constantly outpacing the ability of this sick and bewildered man, who had once been so full of energy and vitality, to react to them. After he won the manipulated presidential election of 1996, we watched the footage of his inauguration and saw how he seemed barely able to walk or talk: it was a grim symbol of the country's own feeble condition.

We had all been excited by the removal of the restrictions that had pinched so many lives during the Soviet Union. There was something intoxicating about the possibilities offered by free elections, a free press and free markets, but at the same time, much of what was described as modernisation consisted simply of repudiating everything that had gone before, and nothing of substance was created to take its place. Nowadays, everyone remembers the queues outside the first branch of McDonald's to be opened in Russia. The restaurant was supposed to be a tangible emblem of change. We were told it was an exemplar of a new world in which you did not need to make friends with the butcher if you wanted a decent cut of meat; the end of the doomed attempt to regulate lives from the centre. Their food smelled and tasted good, it was cheap, the restaurants were colourful and clean, but, ultimately, what they served possessed very little nutritional value. You could say the same about the whole of the country's nascent consumer economy. While luxury goods did flow into the country, very few people could afford them, and the trinkets that were affordable were also low in quality.

People soon began to realise that if you had broken your leg, it mattered little if you owned a pair of Levi's; what was important was that hospitals were so short of funds that they could no longer treat you properly.

And while there had been grumbles about the way that the *nomenklatura* had led gilded existences in the Soviet Union, we soon learned what corruption really meant. I was once told that the difference between business and theft is that thieves steal the investment and split it among themselves, whereas businessmen wait until they have earned a profit before they take any money; thieves do nothing, businessmen finish a project. As I watched, aghast, while Boris Yeltsin and his government oversaw the mass transfer of state assets into the hands of a small number of already wealthy businessmen, I realised that perhaps the distinction between theft and business was not as clear as I had previously thought. In theory, this was all in the name of liberalising the economy and introducing the principles of private ownership, but, like millions of other Russians, I knew a crime when I saw it.

To begin with the people themselves had not known what to make of the huge privatisations that took place during the early '90s. The process itself was foggy and obscure, its vocabulary was full of abstruse technical terms, most of which they had never heard before. It is perhaps telling that the country's first Prime Minister, Yegor Gaidar, was dismissive of the population's ability to understand the changes his government was introducing. He was a youthful economist who was so disdainful of his fellow countrymen's intellectual gifts that he barely made any effort to explain reforms that promised to change their lives completely. This helped contribute to one of the biggest failures of the whole privatisation process – certainly the most emblematic: the vouchers that were intended to give every citizen a stake in the state's assets.

Each voucher corresponded to a portion of the nation's wealth, and it was hoped that they would help encourage the formation of a broad-based middle class who would be the foundation for a democratic Russia. It was unfortunate that these vouchers, issued with a great fanfare to the population in 1992, were undermined from the very start by a profound misjudgement: their value was based on an assessment made in 1984. Back then, 10,000 roubles – the nominal price emblazoned on each voucher – equated to around $16,000 dollars. By 1992, 10,000 roubles was equivalent to just $25. We were told that the voucher would be worth the same as a Volga car, but that misjudgement – combined with hyperinflation on the cost of everyday goods – meant that they were worthless to most people who just needed ready cash to survive.

In theory, distributing these vouchers rather than disposing of the state's assets on the open market was supposed to keep them out of the hands of the mafia and the existing managers – the 'red directors' whose grip on the former state enterprises it was thought essential to break. But the vast majority were easily tempted (or sometimes coerced) into selling, or 'investing', their vouchers by an informed minority who were aware of their true value. It is no surprise, really, they were desperately poor and did not trust these alien, baffling pieces of paper – none of them had read the small print and they did not understand what they actually held in their hands.

Even the process of transforming your voucher into shares was complex, and was often made more so by a number of unscrupulous practices. For instance, although Gazprom's shares were supposedly being issued openly, the majority of them were only made available at a small number of far-flung locations near their centres of operations. It was perfect for insiders, completely inaccessible to anyone else.

I myself managed to get some shares in Gazprom when they were issued in St Petersburg. But even then your ten or fifteen shares counted for nothing in those huge enterprises when the owners of the company could perform a series of what might as well have been conjuring tricks and you had to watch, impotently, as everything you had put in disappeared into somebody else's bulging pockets.

In this time of hucksters, advertising corrupt pyramid schemes and barrels of 'magic' water on television, many just sold their vouchers for instant cash rather than holding out for the dubious prospect of a dividend at some unspecified point in the future. The government's good intentions had been compromised by its fatally flawed implementation, and the state's holdings ended up under the sway of precisely the people that the voucher scheme had been designed to prevent from gaining control of them.

As time went by, the majority of the Russian population came to hate the 'reforms' and everyone connected with them, even more so because they saw others making money off the back of the soaring hyperinflation that had completely eroded their life savings. What did they care about the dogma of free-market economy? All they saw was robbery on the state level. A tiny handful got very rich during this time while millions of ordinary Russians sank further into poverty. It was as if they were saying: 'Rules are for the little people, they do not apply to men like us.'

For my part, I continued for a while to serve in the KGB and then the organisation formed to take its place, the FSB. The security services in Russia were not involved in the tumultuous events of 1991, such as the attempted coup that saw disaffected generals drive their tanks onto the Russian White House lawn. We made no attempts to stop the progress of democracy elsewhere; it was after all the political path that the party had decreed the country should follow. But we still occasionally found ourselves caught up in the rage and tensions that infused every layer of society.

Many of my countrymen were gripped by a feverish icono-clasm in the months after the end of the Soviet Union. It was as if they desperately needed to find some way of transmitting the inchoate feelings of bewilderment and rage this tectonic change had left them with. Across the country, statues commemorating the heroes of communism were hauled to the ground. Outside the Lubyanka[6] in Moscow, a monument to the Cheka's founder Felix Dzerzhinsky was toppled and not long after there was an attempt to do the same to another monument to him in Leningrad. But there was a difference between the two cities. When a group of civilians massed near the statue, ready to smash it to pieces, they were confronted by a handful of officers who braced themselves in front of the stone figure. They were not armed, but made it clear that anybody who tried to do any damage would receive a bloody nose for their efforts. If they wanted to tear a statue down, the officers suggested, it would be better for them to look elsewhere. As it turned out, very few if any of the socialist monuments in Leningrad met the same fate as their counterparts in Moscow – perhaps appropriate, in this traditionally revolutionary city.

We must be careful before we judge the actions of men and women from the past; it is too easy to condescend to history. And we must remember also that when we destroy the artefacts of the previous order, we are depriving future generations of their past: one cannot cut the cord of history in the middle without incurring a terrible loss. Though this is of course the aim of any ideology that wants to achieve complete control over the society in which it finds itself. For the ideology to take root, its adherents must demolish everything to do with the civilisation it has supplanted – and those items for which the population feel most affection are considered the most dangerous, for they represent a challenge to the new ideology's hegemony over the people's

---

6 The popular name for the building that contained the headquarters of the KGB.

hearts and minds. Once already during the twentieth century Russia had seen its cultural and spiritual inheritance smashed, when the Bolsheviks destroyed countless old monuments and churches. In 1991, however, we hoped for stability, and that the values that had inspired the best aspects of the old regime would continue to underpin whatever new society emerged in its aftermath. So we could not accept this symbolic annihilation of everything that the Soviet Union had once represented, which was informed by a blind, vicious fury that wishes only to spit in the eye of the past.

A couple of months later, in the summer of 1991, I was sitting in my office when I got a telephone call, a strange communication that unsettled and reassured me in equal measure. The man on the other end of the line was the vice-director of the Ioffe Physical-Technical Institute, where I had spent some years as a researcher before leaving for New York. He was not a friend – a colleague at most – but nevertheless he said to me:

> You used to work at the institute, I remember you. I know what
> is going on now; I know how witch hunts turn out – if you ever
> need protection, if you ever need a safe house for your family or
> yourself, this is my telephone number, just call me. I have a dacha
> near St Petersburg. You will always be welcome there.

His communication with me was a response to the uncomfortable sequence of events, which began in the summer of 1991, when a decree by Yeltsin suspended the activities of the Communist Party, another step that made me realise that I was vulnerable now in ways I had never considered possible. There had been violence in Estonia, Georgia, Azerbaijan. Even in Czechoslovakia, the site of the bloodless 'Velvet Revolution', the entire senior hierarchy of their secret service had been eliminated – each man gunned down without even the pretence of a trial.

And in Russia, the government had said that the new so-called democrats could enter the KGB premises and were to be given access to any document – cables, records, CVs – they asked for. It was supposed to herald a new openness in society, but instead it simply meant that the many thousands of people who over the past years had, in one form or another, cooperated with the state were suddenly at risk. The principle that we were responsible for our agents had always governed our operations; we could not abandon them now, no matter how much our country had changed. We spent days burning entire files, thrusting sheet after sheet into the furnaces in our office.

The fact that the institute's director had felt compelled to contact me at all was a sign of the curious and dangerous times through which we were living, but his generosity of spirit was a welcome reminder that the best of my country's values were still intact, embodied by men like him. I cherish the memory of that man's goodness; it is as valuable to me as any medal I have ever received. I thank God too that I never had cause to use the number he gave me.

Even before I left the service in 1995, I realised I would have to strain every sinew to ensure that I could carve out a small corner that would allow me to support my family. During my time in the KGB, I had been trained for mimicry; I could be whatever, whoever. I felt as comfortable in black tie and tails as I did in the white laboratory coat of a scientist. Now was the time to see if I could succeed in a different world.

In 1991, along with Yuri Kovalchuk and Andrey and Sergey Fursenko, I had created an organisation called Temp,[7] which we envisaged as a kind of umbrella company that would provide a home for all of the business projects we wanted to pursue – many of which we knew would be in the science and technology sphere – making the most of the contacts and knowledge our relationship with the Ioffe Institute and other similar research facilities had furnished us with. We were trying to do something sustainable, with a moral core, bringing foreign investment and expertise to St Petersburg that would end up being of benefit to the city.

Strange as it may seem to readers thirty years on, profit was not our main goal. We knew it was important if our business was to be a success, and yet we had been brought up to value other things more than money; our priorities were achieving respect and a certain position in society. We also thought it was essential to do something positive. We had received a good education and the people around us thought well of us. In addition to this, my time in the United States had furnished me with a good command of English and experience in dealing with Western-ers. But while these were advantages that set us apart from our competitors, I am not sure that they were enough. When we set up our company it was inevitable we would draw heavily on the ideological precepts that we were used to. We did not understand until later on that there was a new reality and that society was

7 Temp's full name was TOO NTP TEMP. TOO is broadly equivalent to LLP (Limited Lia-
   bility Partnership), and NTP stands for Scientific-Technical Enterprise.

already dashing off in a different direction. It could sometimes feel as if we were trying to perfect the design of the abacus at a time when everybody else was already using calculators.

In this respect, we were different to some of our younger competitors. The generation born in the '60s was more cynical and ruthless, and less convinced that the state had anything to offer them. They did not think anything with public involvement could yield anything worth having. While I grew up in the aftermath of the Khrushchev thaw, in a time that fizzed with possibility, they came of age once its promise had given way to disillusion, and the system had already entered terminal decline. I had experience of a system that worked, but they only knew its flaws. They felt no obligation to provide anything in return.

Our group operated on communal principles, and we essentially lived and worked in each other's pockets – it was more like an Israeli kibbutz than anything. I even included my pension from the secret service as part of the collective's income, something that did not endear me to my wife. But it was important to me, and important for the ethos of our group; we did not feel it was right for one person to be richer than anyone else, so we all received exactly the same proportion of the profits. (In a sense, it could be seen as a continuation of the ways of structuring activity that had emerged in the first enterprises that had been allowed to function in the Soviet Union in the '80s. They were all cooperatives, often with strong ties to organisations like the Komsomol.)

We had lived for years under a planned economy; now we were having to learn how to survive in an improvised one. Nothing about the Marxist economics we had studied so closely equipped us to navigate the challenges that came with running a capitalist enterprise, especially in a country that was falling apart around us. But one of the virtues of operating in such an unstructured, fluid business environment was that you did not feel as if you were in a straitjacket. There were more opportunities, more openings, and if something felt interesting, you could throw yourself into it.

For instance, as well as the more technical projects we pursued under the Temp banner, I was invited, independently, by a foreign investor to help structure the privatisations of two hotels in St Petersburg: Hotel Europa, where I was made a member of the board, and the Hotel Astoria. My colleagues at Temp were initially highly sceptical about this – they saw it as a waste of my time – until they realised how much money it meant I could bring back to invest into our group's activities.

These hotels, which had previously been owned by local government, were among the very first privatisations, so we quickly discovered where the holes in both the nascent legislation and also our own knowledge were. I was there to straighten out their reporting processes, the way in which their budget was created and then approved, and to ensure accountability – though a number of foreign investors had been encouraged to put money in, initially they found themselves completely frozen out of all of the decision-making processes by the director. Effectively, I had been charged with trying to find a way of protecting the interests of both the city and the foreign investors at a time when everyone was trying to accustom themselves to this very new environment. It was very difficult to articulate relations between, say, the municipal authorities, who wanted to keep a portion of shares, and private investors, who did not want any state entities as a shareholder; and also between Russians, who had little experience of investment, and foreigners such as Sir Rocco Forte, who had wanted to put money into the Hotel Astoria. You could see it as a microcosm of debates that were being pursued right across Russia, by people who barely had any experience of capitalism.

Should we allow people from abroad to own parts of Russian businesses? What proportion of a company's shares was enough? What percentage was too much? What ideas and practices from our lives under communism still had some kind of value in this new world? What ideas and practices would we have to jettison? Do we look to import models of privatisation from abroad wholesale? Or do we try and develop a mode of operating more directly tailored to our own specific circumstances? What was an appropriate vocabulary to use when negotiating with other parties?

Success, or otherwise, we soon found, depended on your access to information and, just as importantly, your ability to exploit it. Many people thrived by a strange kind of alchemy: they were able to turn other people's ignorance into gold. For instance, before 1991 there were so few people engaged in entrepreneurial activity that it was easy for local authorities to cope with the administration they generated, but with the fall of communism, a special municipal department had to be created so that they could achieve some measure of control over the registration of the many new businesses that were being established. Despite their best efforts, the whole process could be chaotic and confusing. There was no comprehensive register of firms, and to begin with there were not even any computers; all the paperwork was generated on typewriters. While the documentation was, on the face of it, fairly primitive, you needed to know how to navigate your way around the forms' slightly antiquated structures if you wanted to secure the necessary authorisation. This is where a host of clever companies stepped in: they realised that there were so many people still unfamiliar with even these basic administrative procedures that there was money to be made for those able to prepare the documents in the correct way on your behalf.

If in those days we did not know what a business plan was, at the same time we had a certain amount of common sense, and we discovered that some of the skills we had acquired in the Soviet Union still had a value in the new world. For instance, both Fursenko and Kovalchuk were veterans of the *Buran* shuttle programme, probably the last significant hi-tech project realised in the USSR before its demise. This experience of structuring and managing complex multi-disciplinary ventures would prove invaluable. And I still remember the first money I earned for our group: US$250,000. Payment for a consultancy report a client had asked me to prepare. I had never written one of these before, but my time in the security services had given me an impeccable grounding in how to write reports. While what I sent to the client may not have looked like the kind of document he was used to receiving from consultants, he was surprised by how rigorous, well sourced and clear the information I provided him was.

We did not conduct market research, and there was not the same army of consultants and business experts out there on hand to give business advice (and, of course, charge you for the privilege). But, again, we applied the principles and knowledge we'd acquired as part of our life experience. This is one of the reasons why so many former KGB officers would go on to thrive in these unfamiliar conditions. We were accustomed, for instance, to evaluating evidence, to problem-solving, to matching answers to questions. Just as significantly, as field officers we had all had a long association with risk, long enough that it had become something akin to a natural condition for many of us. We knew what it felt like to exist in a climate of instability; we had all spent months working on an operation only to see it disrupted at the last minute by a completely unexpected turn of events. We knew what it meant to be at the mercy of chance, so we were prepared to respond to it in a positive, pragmatic fashion. When you added this to the wide range of connections, both among former colleagues and the scientific community, that we had formed during our careers, then you can see how well set we were.

Our success with water filters in St Petersburg was a case in point. We had been alerted to the fact that water in the city was barely potable (the water-cleaning stations had been closed; another unfortunate result of the collapse of the country's infrastructure), and we were aware of a particular mineral that could purify the water very effectively. While you could already buy water filters in any of the small department stores across the city, our connection to the research institutes gave us a technological advantage – nobody else had any knowledge about this mineral, whereas we knew where to obtain it and how to use it. Most importantly, we were confident that it could be done cheaply and that it would bring us a healthy profit. We had strong connections with the scientists working in research institutes, as well as an intellectual background that meant we were able to recognise the value and significance of their discoveries. We were accustomed to thinking nimbly, to responding to local conditions, to identifying opportunities and then making the most of them. It was not market research in the sense that an MBA student might understand it, but intuitively we reached the same conclusions as might a company who had commissioned acres of research.

Eventually we were able to use the knowledge of the Russian business environment we were acquiring as the basis for a consultancy project we established in the International Centre for Business Cooperation, the imitation of the World Trade Center we set up in St Petersburg. We rented office space to foreign companies, as well as providing advice on Russian rules and laws and the prevailing conditions, and effecting introductions to local businesses.

I can see now, with the benefit of two decades of hindsight, how flawed the whole trade centre project was. It bore no relation to the kind of endeavour someone who had been to a business school would have embarked on. Our ambition was to help attract Western companies (and the expertise they possessed) to St Petersburg, but we had only the vaguest sense of how to achieve this. We would learn that being aware of the existence of the World Trade Center in New York, and having a basic understanding of how it operated, did not translate into anything that resembled a strategy. We had no comprehensive business plan, we never set out long-term targets for how much we needed to earn if we were to carry on trading. We thought that it would simply be enough to open our doors, offer basic services such as cleaning, security and consulting, and then foreign businesses and money would flood in. I barely gave profit a thought, at least until the day our partners demanded a return on their investment and I realised I would have to run around like a madman if I was to repay them. Suddenly having 5,000-odd square metres of empty floorspace on our hands did not seem like a very good idea. After a good deal of work I was able to strike a deal with a pair of businessmen who I'd already had some exchanges with previously, Vladimir Potanin and Mikhail Prokhorov, who leased space in the trade centre for their fledgling Onexim Bank. This bought us the time we needed.

It would be difficult to overstate how provisional our arrangements were. Staff were generally recruited in a fairly unceremonious fashion, usually via a personal connection. You might remember someone whom you'd worked with before, or a friend would hear that you were looking for a new secretary and suggest someone they knew. We did not have proper contracts; instead we would create a letter of employment that simply confirmed the individual's job title and salary. And our staff were all paid in cash; it would be a long time before anyone was set up with the capacity to pay their employees by BACS, or even by cheque.

Temp was organised on similar lines. We did not have any written agreements stipulating how much each of us was owed at a particular time, or how much of the business we owned. Instead, when we met we would have a discussion and then agree what sum we would each be paid. The International Centre for Business Cooperation was actually a joint venture between us and two Israeli citizens, but we did not draw up a formal agreement; the whole enterprise was essentially founded on a handshake.

We used similar informal channels to find customers and

investors. The better connected you were, the better your chances of securing capital or business opportunities. Access to political contacts in particular was hugely important; indeed, it would be possible to argue that if you did not possess these then your enterprise was doomed before it had taken its first step. Precisely because the Soviet state had such far-reaching influence in every corner of life, those people who had previously worked within it possessed an enormous range of connections and influence. You could use former state officials to help you with practical issues such as banking and registration, but where they excelled was their ability to pick up the phone and make contact with others who might be useful, whether as clients, investors, customers, partners or suppliers.

What was also significant in this context was that, in a country in which the rule of law had collapsed, where neither business nor individuals were protected by the kinds of safeguards we now take for granted, these former officials could act as guarantors of your integrity. It is difficult to understand the extent to which trust underpins any business transaction unless you have seen what it is like to try and work in an environment where there were no tribunals to settle disputes, no means of redress if you had been cheated. There were criminals everywhere. As soon as they could smell money on somebody they would descend on them, demanding 'protection' money, making them offers they could not refuse. If, on the other hand, you had been vouched for by a man who until recently had been a senior party boss or an officer in either law enforcement or the special services, then it meant that potential investors knew you were somebody they could do business with. You could call it an alternative economy of trust.

We certainly benefited greatly from our connections both in the secret services and the scientific community. As much as anything else, a huge number of transactions originated from word-of-mouth recommendations. For instance, one day in 1991 I received a call from a friend of mine, who knew I'd been part of a scientific research institute. He told me that there was a director of a state-owned military factory who needed to dispose of a highly valuable quantity – 900 kilos, a substantial amount – of germanium, a semiconductor material, but that he was worried it could potentially fall into the hands of the bandits who circled those enterprises like vultures. Many were far less scrupulous than this guy; where he tried to dispose of his surplus in a responsible way, others would have simply sold the materials to the first crook who knocked on their door, and pocketed the profit.

I'd never been involved in something like this before, but then that was true of pretty much any business transaction one entered into at the time, so I agreed to meet the director. He said to me, 'Listen, I don't really care what price you end up paying for this material, but you were recommended to me as an experienced and decent person, so I feel I can rely completely on you.'

Because of the conference I had attended in Malaga all those years previously, and my work at the Ioffe Institute, I already understood something of the qualities germanium possessed. And though there was not an established market for it, after speaking to a few friends from the scientific community I came to understand that we would be able to sell it for a substantial price. We then discovered that because it was a substance used in laser technology, it needed to be given a 'passport' by a special laboratory, otherwise it would be worthless. Again we called upon scientist friends, who helped us find a laboratory in Moscow who could provide the necessary certification.

Next, I found a buyer who offered a price far in excess of what I had anticipated, though I knew that I was far from being home and dry. There is a famous Russian anecdote about two guys who meet in the road. 'Hey,' says the first man, 'I want to buy a wagon of sugar. Do you know anyone who might be willing to sell me one?' 'That's strange,' says the other guy, 'I just happen to have a wagon of sugar I need to shift.' Flushed by this happy coincidence, they waste no time in reaching a deal. As soon as they shake hands, the second man sprints off to find a wagon of sugar and the first guy runs in the opposite direction to try and rustle up the cash to buy it.

I was in almost precisely the same situation. Luckily, I was able to persuade the vendor to sign a contract committing to deliver the germanium two days before I paid him. I then arranged a deal with the buyer agreeing that he would pay me two days in advance of the goods. This bought me four days in which the staff in the laboratory worked like hell, day and night, to issue all the necessary documentation.

In many ways, this exchange exemplified how so many business deals at the time were conducted. It was precisely Russia's volatility that made it attractive to foreign investors – it was regarded as a country where you could turn small sums into large fortunes – and plenty of others made a living out of this kind of arrangement, flying by the seats of their pants, but also carving out lucrative existences as middlemen. I made a substantial amount of money – 14 million roubles, if I remember correctly – from the germanium deal, but I knew that in the long run this kind of operation was not for me. I wanted to improve my knowledge, skills and understanding. I wanted to build and create.

My time at Temp came to an end when in 1998 I received a call from my friend Vladimir Putin, who was deputy chief of Yeltsin's Presidential Administration. Putin, who I had known for a number of years by this point, knew that the idealistic spirit that had guided Temp from the beginning had started to sour a little, and that I would need little persuading to return to the government apparatus. He proposed a role that he thought I would be suitable for. 'I suppose it is time for you to change your occupation,' he said to me. 'An opportunity has arisen. What do you think? If you agree, I can submit your CV.'

I would continue as a member of the Temp cooperative for a while longer, but my career as an active businessman was over, at least for a while. Huge numbers of people had rushed to join the ranks of new entrepreneurs during the '90s, but not many lasted long. Even at Temp, with all the advantages we had, two thirds of the enterprises we began failed and very few things ever turned out the way we planned. But we were lucky that the other third was successful enough to subsidise the rest of our activities, and give us a decent standard of living. When we sold them, endeavours like the business centre made us a healthy profit. We had become a highly respected, prominent organisation. Civil servants were even sent to my office to be taught something of business and management.

Nevertheless, in 1998 I divested myself of both the successful enterprises and those projects that had never quite fulfilled the hopes we had of them – such as the Rossiya Bank, the bank formerly owned by the CPSU – and returned to working for the state.

Perhaps it was too romantic of me to assume that Temp could continue to work and live according to the principles we set out to follow; after all, even Israeli kibbutzim can fail to survive. But I am proud that I never wrecked anybody's business, or anybody's belongings, and I never let anybody down. We made money and we contributed something to society.

It is only now, over two decades on, that I have come to see those men from the Russian Communist Workers' Party differently. They were poor, stubborn creatures unaware of their own obsolescence, though in their persistence there was a kind of melancholic dignity. But what I did not see then, what none of us saw, was that, unwittingly or not, they were a valuable reminder that, over the past century, we Russians have sometimes been so eager to usher in new ways of running our world that we have completely discarded everything that existed before. The baby goes out with the bath water, and whatever is good and valuable is lost along with the cruelty and the dross. But no ideological programme ever survives contact with the real world, no matter how seductive or complete its promises might appear. That Russia has been the graveyard of many utopias in its history is something that we all would have done well to bear in mind. How different things could have been.

CHAPTER FOUR

THE FROST, THE DEEP
NIGHT, THE SNOW
AND THE ICE

It is said that people who have suffered an amputation are vulnerable to feeling phantom sensations in the empty space where their limbs used to be. They will try to pick something up with an arm that is no longer there, or attempt to scratch an itch on a leg that disappeared years ago. Most often, they feel pain. I sometimes think of this phenomenon when I consider the end of the Soviet Union. I am not naïvely nostalgic, I do not yearn to see the hammer and sickle flag flying again, and yet still I feel a nagging sense of loss.

The end of the Soviet Union meant the creation of a new border between Georgia and Russia, but many of us continued to regard the two nations simply as different parts of the same country. For three centuries we had fought and suffered alongside each other, we maintain many of the same traditions, and there are as many Georgians in Moscow as you might find strolling around the streets of Tbilisi. But after 1991, it was too easy for some to forget these shared bonds and in the summer of 2008, against a background of deteriorating relations between Georgia and Russia, gunfire and bloodshed returned to Transcaucasia, a region that had clung for years to a fragile peace settlement. The place of most intense fighting was in South Ossetia.

As you might expect, official communications between the two nations had been completely cut – even diplomats were no longer talking to each other – but despite this, the call I received on my mobile phone from Irakli Ezugbaia, the head of the Georgian railways, was not at all surprising. There was a long tradition of warm, constructive cooperation between our two networks, a legacy of the creation, almost immediately after the dissolution of the USSR, of the Union of Railways of CIS countries (made up of the former Soviet republics). It was decided then that the railways of the post-Soviet republics should work using the same regulations and share decisions on trans-border operations, with the head of the Russian railway system as chairman. The farsighted people behind the union knew that if every country introduced its own legislation and changes, the result would be chaos. It was an arrangement that had worked incredibly well for seventeen years, and one that we had seen endure even at moments of profound regional tension. Indeed, I would argue that the union helped promote constructive relationships among its members. (Though, for instance, Georgia left the CIS after the 2008 conflict, it remained an associated member of the CIS railway union.)

'I am speaking to you as one professional to another, and would like to ask a question,' Ezugbaia said to me. I could tell he was feeling awkward, because under the circumstances he had no idea how I would react. In polite, tense tones, he told me that they only had one week's worth of grain stored in Tbilisi and that they were waiting anxiously for a transport of foodstuffs from Kazakhstan. The train would have to cross Russian territory, using our rail infrastructure. Could I permit it? he asked.

My immediate feeling was that, irrespective of the circumstances, the transit should continue. If we stopped it, then not only might there be severe humanitarian consequences, but we risked destroying the whole structure of the railway union. However, at the same time I knew that under the circumstances it would have been completely inappropriate for me to take a unilateral decision. Railways are not governments – their responsibility is not to make final decisions on foreign policy, but to carry passengers and cargo in comfort and safety – and so I said I would raise the matter with the Kremlin. A little while later, Prime Minister Putin (as he was then) called me and asked me to give him my opinion on the matter; what did I think should be done? Once I had explained the circumstances to him, and given him my assessment of the likely consequences if we stopped the transport, he ended the call – a little while later the grain was on its way to Tbilisi. The next time I saw the Georgian railway president, he simply said, 'Thank you very much.' It was a routine solution to a crisis situation in which two professionals had cooperated in the way that two professionals should. We did not even raise a glass in celebration.

You see, I always considered that, if you stripped away everything else, I only had one task: the railways should run efficiently and effectively. Even during the civil war in Ukraine, although officially communications between Russia and Ukraine had been severed (Russian Railways lost 50 per cent of its passenger business in one fell swoop), Russia and the breakaway region of the Donbass continued to send coal by train to Kiev.

But if the rail networks that Russia inherited after the fall of the Soviet Union were remarkably resilient, there were other respects in which the settlements made in 1991 left my country vulnerable, weak and ill-prepared to build a new nation up from the ashes of communism. It was as if our body had been dismembered, and for years to come, that loss would continue to cause us great pain, even if we would later learn that some of the agony we felt was only a phantom sensation.

By the mid-1990s Russia was still struggling to get on its feet. The state was weaker than it had been at any point since the Civil War. It had lost 50 per cent of its industrial capacity, opponents – from both inside and outside the country – circled it, actively supporting chaos and instability, and the plummeting price of oil tore great holes in the government's budget.

Russia's entire political system had been crippled, which meant that in turn the entire legal system had collapsed too. I witnessed a great deal in my role as head of the North-West Inspectorate of the Chief Control Directorate of the President, an institution that was established in 1991 to ensure that presidential decrees were implemented and, once the process had begun, to provide a degree of oversight (something Russia had never had before). You could describe us as the President's watchdog.

The rule people lived by was as follows: if it was not expressly prohibited, then you could consider it permitted (echoing Gorbachev's Law on Cooperatives, an ostensibly modest document that contained a ticking time bomb). The legal system had had to be retooled to allow it to be able to regulate the new Russia, but, inevitably, given that the political, social and economic landscapes seemed to be changing by the second, the redrafting of legislation left many gaps. So Yeltsin had to constantly issue decrees to close loopholes or resolve anomalies. The problem was exacerbated by the fact that the accounts chamber of the Duma (the equivalent to the British Treasury's audit committee) was poorly organised and toothless – by comparison, the Directorate was far stronger. There was no doubt that we were needed. When I started, approximately 50 per cent of Yeltsin's orders were being ignored or going unfulfilled. The Soviet Union had been dissolved over half a decade ago, and yet still the state's ability to actually govern remained perilously weak.

It was not just that it did not feel as if the state could pro-tect or support the people any more – those who were supposed to be running the country actually gave a good impression of being more interested in filling their own pockets. We created monsters during that era; and we fed them, too. They became fat and strong off Russia's flesh and blood. When today I hear how some officials in the Putin administration are being criticised for corruption, for having improperly obtained 2 million roubles, I want desperately to remind them that tens of trillions were stolen during the '90s – 'appropriated' by the so-called Democrats and Liberals, shapeshifters who lauded the state one moment, and the next were demanding that it should be reformed out of existence. They were the men who were lionised in the West because, by making all the right noises about introducing a market economy, they were perceived to be behaving correctly. They were privatis-ing state-owned property (it was the largest transfer of state assets into private hands in history, and it was not just industries like gas and oil – it was everything: bakeries, hairdressers, biscuit makers); they were forming new cadres of leaders; they were sweeping away the crumbling dead remnants of the Soviet system. But nobody bothered to ensure that the key laws and institutions of a market were established first, or to assess whether the Russian population was ready for the onslaught of red-blooded capitalism.

Who cared about the impact on society? Who cared if it would lead to a stark rise in criminality? Who cared about the disenfranchisement of the vast majority of the people who knew, in the marrow of their bones, that they were being excluded from this process? An invisible hand would look after us all, or at least that is what we were informed by the Western advisers who had flooded into the country to tell us how to run our lives.

I saw men who claimed to be democrats coming to power, and saw too how they spent their time trying to acquire as many assets as possible, and by whatever means necessary. I remember one case in which someone who was very highly placed in Yeltsin's administration visited the director of a former state enterprise and demanded, in no uncertain terms, that he should give up the shares he held in the company (it should be said that the means by which the director himself had come by them were also open to question). When the director refused, he was simply thrown into jail on trumped-up charges. One of his first visitors was the very same person who had tried to persuade him to part with his shares in the first place. Perhaps he would like to reconsider his position? They were relentless in their pursuit of personal gain. Relentless.

It was made worse by the fact that crooks infested every layer of the bureaucracy, operating behind a façade of legality. They oc-cupied administrative positions, which they swiftly discovered they could turn into fiefdoms of their own in which they could exist un-touched, like miniature emperors. Moscow was so feeble, so remote, that orders or instructions emanating from government represent-atives appeared to those in the provinces like tiny blips on a radar that had no impact on their business. For that kind of man, the only authority that counted was the pistol they kept in their drawers.

During the early '90s, I had been nominated by the then mayor of St Petersburg Anatoly Sobchak to join the board of the Baltic Shipping Company, which had formerly been the engine of the Soviet Union's 'window to the West' – transporting Soviet goods and passengers to capitalist countries – but was now facing huge, overwhelming problems. Organised crime, representatives of the federal government and regional politicians were all fighting over its wounded body, and somehow I was supposed to try and pro-tect the interests of the city. Two years after I became involved, the chairman of the board was shot dead in broad daylight by bandits who wanted to seize control.

Since I was still then an officer in the secret services and had the right to carry arms (there were plenty of people who did not have that privilege, but who swaggered around with one anyway), I hid my pistol in a holster under my jacket. I developed a habit when I was out and about with my wife, for instance coming back from the theatre: I would instinctively move my right hand to hover over where the weapon was concealed. After a while, Natalia no-ticed that I seemed always to be clutching the left-hand side of my chest. Disturbed, she looked me in the eye and told me in no uncertain terms that if I had any problems with my heart I should visit the doctor immediately. It is funny now, but that was not a normal way to live; life in Russia had become pathological.

Of course, the criminals were clever enough to realise that there were better ways for them to do business than just gunning men down in the street. They seemed to have an almost boundless ability to corrupt people, and an almost limitless number of men who were willing to be corrupted. And if you are going to try and weasel your way into the system, why not go straight to the top?

Around that time, I became acquainted with Dmitry Shakhanov, a bright young officer who was the deputy head of a special police division dedicated to fighting organised crime. In the normal course of his work, he detained a number of crooks who happened to have close links with a senior St Petersburg official. The official was incandescent. He demanded that his friends should be released, and when Shakhanov refused to comply, the official resolved instead to destroy his career. Within two, at most three, months, Shakhanov had been fired from the police on entirely spurious charges, and the official was not finished there; it was clear that he would not stop until he had ensured that the only job Shakhanov would ever be able to do again would be one cleaning the streets. Instead, I invited him to work for me at the Directorate. I knew it would do nothing for my popularity with the official, but I knew too that because I was absolutely independent from the local authorities, there was nothing he could say or do to prevent me. Still, to see how the lowest elements of society had embroidered themselves into the fabric of government, where they could operate with impunity, left a sour taste in my mouth.

And their days are not done yet. A couple of years ago I received an email, sent, I suppose, from hell. It seemed to be an unsettling coda to a case that I had been involved with in St Petersburg in which I had helped put a notorious criminal behind bars: a man who I knew had long since breathed his last. 'You, bloody Vladimir Yakunin,' it read, 'you cracked the life of an honourable person, you will pay for this.' I still do not know who sent it.

Sometimes, the most serious crimes occurred where no blood was spilled. We were called to investigate activity at the Baltic Shipyard, which at that time was engaged in building the cruiser *Peter the Great*. The construction process, which had begun almost a decade previously, had been long and complex, but now, for reasons that were not immediately clear, it had shuddered to a halt. We began to make a forensic study of their records, and the further in we got, the more obvious it became that if construction was not completed then a criminal investigation would have to be initiated to discover what had gone wrong.

As the head of the Directorate, I had the authority to send letters to any federal service or territory throughout the north-west. We could demand to see representatives of whomever we were investigating, and could call on the support of the Ministry of Internal Affairs and the tax office, but, ultimately, there were limits to our authority. Because we were not a law enforcement office, we had no other powers of compulsion, so all we could do was dig into the situation as deeply as we were able and then provide the documents to the administration and the President. The problem was that 50 million roubles were needed to finish the work on this state-of-the-art ship. If it stayed another month in the shipyard, then all its major systems would go beyond their guarantees and it would have to be completely renovated and reconstructed. Ten years of work, ten years of enormous investment, would be compromised all because of the mendacity of a handful of criminals.

I wrote a letter to our Moscow headquarters asking President

Yeltsin to provide 50 million roubles from his special Reserve Fund to finish the ship, which he duly supplied. So, in a sense, the episode was resolved in a relatively straightforward fashion, but to me it spoke so loudly about the way that the country had become almost unrecognisable in only a matter of years. That this ship could have been subject to the predations of these vultures, that people had become so oblivious to the pressing demands of our national security, and inured to a consideration of national pride, showed me that something had been lost since the fall of the Soviet Union. I did not like the chaos and cynicism that had rushed in to fill the void it had left.

I have heard it said that without access to the Baltic ports, Russia would disappear into the frost, the deep night, the snow and the ice. You do not need to compete with Russia in an arms race; it is enough just to deprive her of her ports. It was with this principle in mind that the port of St Petersburg, which was to give Russia access to the Baltic trade routes, was originally constructed. It was an ambition with a history almost as old as Russia itself. During the reign of Ivan the Third, the Hanseatic League explored the possibility of building ports along the south coast of the Gulf of Finland, and a few centuries later Peter the Great's determination to build the country's principal port here was frustrated only by the region's shallow waters. However, after the Great Patriotic War, once Estonia and Latvia were absorbed into the Soviet Union, more than a trillion dollars was invested into building the transport infrastructure of the Baltic republics instead, notably two of what were at the time among the most modern ports in the world: Tallinn in Estonia and Ventspils in Latvia. When these vital assets fell into the hands of the new independent republics, Russia was in danger once more of being condemned to a reliance on the transport infrastructure of another nation. Only then did the dangers inherent in a policy of prioritising the development of Ventspils and Tallinn become apparent.[8]

At a stroke, the country had lost its access to world markets and severely hampered its prospects of economic development. It had other ports, but they were concentrated in remote locations and were either ice-bound for large stretches of the year or given over to military use. There was a decent port at St Petersburg, but it only possessed a relatively shallow channel (the direct result of a decision taken in the '70s to privilege the modernisation of the Baltic ports), and could not support visits from high-tonnage ships. The loss of Russia's delivery channels was all the more severe at a time when its economy's growth was fuelled by raw materials such as coal and fertilisers that in the main had to be transported via seaports. There was also an agonising emotional shock, especially for those who, like me, had personal connections to the Baltic states. I had spent the first fourteen years of my life in Estonia. When I was growing up, the idea that this bond might be severed would have been inconceivable. And what made it sadder was that, following independence, an ugly brand of nationalism had emerged in

---

8 At the infamous December 1991 meeting at the CPSU Central Committee's dacha deep in the forest of Belovezhskaya Pushcha in Belarus at which the dissolution of the Soviet Union was made official, Sobchak told Yeltsin that if he was going to sign the agreement – already by this point three of the Baltic republics had seceded unilaterally – then he should also ensure that he sat down with the leaders of the newly independent countries and discuss exactly what territory should be assigned to which nation, and also the terms that would apply for Russia's continued use of strategic assets such as the Baltic ports. This never happened. (Though the responsibility was not Yeltsin's alone – those men who had taken control of the nascent republics of, for instance, Latvia and Estonia avoided this important discussion.)

each of these countries. Bruised by this surge of unprecedented rancour, we learned a new lesson: politics is not aesthetic – it tramples over people's feelings and does not care how it looks as long as it achieves its aims.

In 1993, Boris Yeltsin issued a presidential decree stating that a port should be built at Ust-Luga, a fishing village that perched beside the Gulf of Finland (it was one of several locations earmarked for development as ports, including Primorsk, Vyborg and Vysotsk, among others). The immediate priority was to support the Russian coal industry (though the terminals were expected to be able to handle other cargo too, such as oil, chemical goods and containers), but the wider geo-political implications were obvious. When 80 per cent of Russia's vital exports – and thus a huge proportion of the nation's GDP – went through the Baltic ports, it simply could not afford to be dependent on the goodwill of a third party to be able to ship its products abroad; this project would help to begin rebuilding the infrastructure of a country that had had many of its strategic assets amputated overnight.[9]

A company called AOOT Kompaniya Ust-Luga ('JSC

---

9   In addition to establishing Ust-Luga as a significant entrepôt for exports, we would later be charged with the development of a ferry route that would provide a stable connection between mainland Russia and the exclave of Kaliningrad, the home of our Baltic Fleet. There is no way of approaching Kaliningrad by land that would not involve crossing 300km of the territory of at least two other nations – Lithuania and Poland are its immediate neighbours, with Latvia, Belarus and Ukraine forming a belt around them.

Because the exclave's residents live under the constant threat of isolation, the quality of its sea connections is thus paramount. The gravity of this situation was underlined in 2001 when the Lithuanian government revoked the overflight rights of the region's sole carrier, Kaliningrad Air, which could afford to neither pay the fees it owed to Lithuania's air-traffic control organisation, nor modernise its fleet to comply with EU safety standards. If the region were cut off, for whatever reason, it would not only have a substantial personal and economic impact, but there would also be severe consequences for its security. How else, other than by ferry, would we be able to transport men and munitions to defend our territory?

No purely commercial entity was ever likely to be persuaded to take this project on – its value lay in its strategic importance. There was never any suggestion it would be a money-spinner, and so, following the initial instructions from the president, the service began running in 2006.

Ust-Luga') was created to begin work in building the port, though initially there was no private investment. Five years later, in 1998, I was called upon to investigate what kind of progress had been made in accordance with Yeltsin's decree. I found nothing. Millions of roubles – some from the state, some from private entrepreneurs, some in the form of a loan from the World Bank – had disappeared into the projects; all they had to show for it were some nicely wrapped plans. We stood there, looking in disbelief at the empty expanse of bleak earth where a port should have been. There was only a single terminal at Ust-Luga, and little more. Worse still, the sea around it was infested with lethal mines that were left over from the Great Patriotic War. What had happened was not criminal as such (for the kind of gangster who wanted to earn as much as he could, as fast as he could, the margins involved and the amount of work it would have needed were too small to be of interest), but something had plainly gone wrong. Once my auditors had provided me with more information, I moved quickly to try and establish what exactly had happened. It became clear that the company had experienced profound, unanticipated difficulties in attracting capital investment, and that the project had been hobbled both by jurisdictional feuding between competing regional authorities and poor management, as well as the fact that there were few if any people around who had experience of large infrastructure projects. Who was to blame, and how could the situation be resolved?

Traditionally, we would assemble everyone involved around a table and then they could elaborate on the shortcomings and problems associated with their respective areas of responsibility. The problem was that there was no sign of Valery

Serdyukov, the deputy governor of Leningrad Oblast, who in theory was responsible for ensuring that the decree was fulfilled. After five minutes I called his office to ask where he had got to. They told me that he was busy somewhere in a very distant district of this vast region, which covered an area roughly the size of France.

Just before I slammed the telephone down, I very calmly informed his secretary that unless Mr Serdyukov appeared before me by 7 p.m. that day, I would be waiting for him the following morning with his letter of resignation, all ready to be delivered to the administration of the President. Within five minutes, a very friendly-sounding Serdyukov called me from God knows where, trying to explain why it had been so important for him to travel to the middle of nowhere that day. I was as calm as I had been earlier with his secretary, and simply told him that I understood his position, but that there was a procedure that needed to be adhered to. I finished by reminding him that I would be waiting until seven; I did not need to say any more.

Which made it all the more surprising when, the following year, 1999, Serdyukov was elected as the governor of the region, and almost the first thing he did was to call and inform me that he had a proposal to put to me. He told me how the pressure to oversee the development of the ports sat heavily on his shoulders, and he needed desperately to find someone else to share the load. Would I be interested in becoming chairman of the board of JSC Ust-Luga? I thought it was an absolutely crazy idea, and wasted no time in telling him so. As much as anything else, I pointed out, as a civil servant I could not become embroiled in running a business venture.

But he would not take no for an answer. I wonder now whether he was invoking the Russian tradition that the man who initiates an idea should also be the man to implement it – had I been less vocal in my assessment of Ust-Luga, perhaps everything would have been different. Serdyukov pushed and pushed until finally I told him that if he wanted a definitive response, he should speak to Alexander Voloshin, who at the time was the head of the presidential administration. Whatever Mr Voloshin ordered me to do, I said to Serdyukov, I would obey immediately. Five days later, I received a telegram signed by Mr Voloshin. It stated that the administration had agreed to nominate me to be the chairman of the board of the Ust-Luga company. My fate was sealed.

I would be working, I was informed, with Mr Serdyukov himself (who would go on to become a brilliant advocate for the port projects at Ust-Luga and Primorsk, with which I would also come to be involved; and a staunch supporter of our board's plans at both local and federal levels), Lyubov Sovershayeva, his deputy, as well as Valery Izrailit, the entrepreneur who had acquired the rights to develop the project. He had been given them as collateral by the entrepreneur who had originally held them – Ilya Baskin, who had had a somewhat chequered business career – and when the loan defaulted, he was keen to make the most of what he had been left with. (When I think back on it, it seems insane that such a massive endeavour could have rested on such a flimsy legal basis: no documents, no notarised contracts; just a conversation between two men. But that is how things were done at the time. If you could not live with that uncertainty, you would never be able to achieve anything.)

The combined efforts of the board, in addition to the support provided by the then Minister of Transport Sergei Frank and his successor Igor Levitin, created an environment in which a unique construction plan could emerge, one which marked a decisive shift in the conception and direction of the project. What we were doing, without knowing anything of the theory, was developing what is now probably one of the best examples of PPP (public–private partnership) in infrastructure in the world.

Ultimately, the arrangement, in which the Ministry of Transport, the Ministry of Railways, local government and our own company were all involved, was an acknowledgement of the fact that in a country facing as many fundamental economic, political and social problems as Russia was at the time, a new path, one which was neither purely private nor public, but a collaboration between the two, was necessary if anything on this scale was to be achieved. Whatever the attempts by the liberal reformers to demonstrate otherwise, the state still had a fundamental role to play in the infrastructure projects that were needed to help drag Russia back up onto its feet.

Usually, newly formed companies follow a fairly well-established path: the board of directors is responsible for the creation of a strategic plan, which is then submitted for the approval of the shareholders, and then handed down to management for implementation and execution. They generally meet twice a year, four times in some cases. But for us it was different. After all, the reality we faced admitted little room for the accepted Western rules of corporate governance. Our shareholders were both private individuals and the state – a situation unfamiliar to us all. We had to seek approval from the Ministry of Transport, and from the moment our plans were accepted we were meeting constantly.

We worked like hell because we knew how complex the project was, how profound some of the challenges facing us were, how many interested parties there were, and how many obstacles were likely to be thrown into our path by people anxious to impede its progress. It seemed like every day a new problem would emerge and we'd have to deal with it as quickly as we could. Some of the land we need is owned by the Ministry of Defence? OK, get them on the phone and let's talk. There's a disagreement between the regional and federal governments about who the new infrastructure we were building should belong to? Fine, we need to draw up new legislation to cover the ownership. Day after day. It was relentless. In fact, we worked so hard that I became possessed, and found it almost impossible to switch off when I got home. Sometimes, my wife would have to say to me: 'Listen, *hello there*, you are not at the office. Please calm down, take a rest.'

I was desperate to learn. I became, once again, the boy who swallowed books whole, who studied so hard that his parents had to force him to go out and skate at the ice rink. I had to educate myself, all over again, about huge subjects such as macro-economics, and complex and highly focused ones such as innovations in loading technology, warehousing and freight processing. We made the acquaintance of leading experts in the field and we travelled constantly, the length and breadth of Europe, even during our holidays. We would come back from almost every visit equipped with a piece of knowledge that was completely new to us: in Germany we'd see how port schemes could belong to the local government rather than disappearing into the hands of private investors; in Rotterdam we'd learn about new automatic systems for processing containers.

Mr Izrailit was so hungry for any knowledge that he thought might give us a technological advantage that he travelled to China to see how similar projects had been conducted there. Even now, a decade or more later, there are few Russian coal ports using equipment as advanced as what you can find at Ust-Luga, something that has been a decisive element in the port's ultimate success. So, for instance, Ust-Luga is now one of the few ports in the world to be equipped with a transporter supply of railcars for unloading, and our scheme for unloading and storing coal was unprecedented in its ability to reduce the process's environmental cost (we spray the coal with mist to suppress the dust).

And it was not just a question of introducing new technology; we also had much to learn about how best to secure the necessary finance for such a complex and expensive endeavour. One of Izrailit's cleverest innovations was to break up the project as a whole into a number of parcels. This meant that what might previously have been seen by potential investors as an impossibly large risk (there were few if any companies or individuals willing or able to commit to the astronomical sum of $2 billion) suddenly became a far more approachable proposition.

Perhaps that was one of the few advantages in having to build from the ground up: we could learn from others' mistakes. We saw what had worked, and what had not, and watched how other nations had balanced the interests of the public with the priorities of private entrepreneurs – it was the best kind of university.

One problem that stared out at us as soon as we began studying the way the ports were functioning in the Baltic republics was they were all free economic zones, with tax breaks for the private companies operating out of them, which obviously made them incredibly attractive to investors, and far cheaper to use. It was my responsibility to try and secure the same advantages for our project. But no matter how hard I tried, no matter how fiercely I argued, the Ministry of Finance would not agree. They put up a concrete wall, hid behind it, and refused to accept the idea of offering a reduced rate to potential investors. They just saw it as lost income. Eventually we managed to persuade the regional government to offer tax incentives, which was something, but it was never sufficient to allow us to compete on a level playing field with the Baltic countries.

Business in Russia at that moment was growing wildly, like an abandoned garden. It was full of energy, but nobody could control it and, because of that, a lot of tricky, predatory things were going on. There was an assumption that the Ust-Luga development would be another one of the quasi-criminal privatisations that we had all seen too many times before. In this scenario, the state would build the port and then hand it over for a nominal price to greedy investors, who could then cash in.

We made it crystal-clear from the very start that nobody would be getting any part of this port for free – after all, the state had already made a substantial investment, which they wanted to be paid back. So if investors wanted a place at the table, they had to enter at a fair market price. And, just as importantly, they also had to commit to the programme of investment that we were proposing. Essentially, while the state would pay for (and retain ownership over) the deep-sea channel and the piers, as well as responsibility for safety and regulation, the rest of the burden had to be shouldered by the private companies. They had to be willing to invest in the development of the roads, the railways, the electricity, the whole infrastructure, and also to guarantee that they would be able to secure the volume of traffic that they had promised in their original bid.

Crucially, JSC Ust-Luga, as port developer, also held a 25 per cent blocking share in each investment project, and would only pay its portion of the costs after the completion of construction. This meant we could ensure that everything proceeded in a co-ordinated fashion. If we had not done so, there was the danger that the entire plan of the port would disintegrate into small pieces. It was essential that, through us, the state retained central control.

In practice this meant that every rouble invested by the government was matched by five roubles of private money. While all around us it seemed as if the state was being systematically stripped of its assets, we were building a crucial element in the nation's economic infrastructure – one that could have substantial implications for both its wealth and security – at minimal cost to the public purse. In fact, most subsequent PPP Russian projects – notably St Petersburg's North-West Orbital and the St Petersburg to Moscow Highway – have been based on legislation drawn up for Ust-Luga.

But investors are beholden to shareholders, not the greater good of society, and our stringent terms meant that although there were many companies who wanted to take control of the existing terminal in Ust-Luga, there was only one that I could actually persuade to pay for it. We saw a lot of potential investors come in with the same attitude: if I'm putting the money in, then I'm the owner and everyone else can go to hell. They chose not to take their interest any further. I guess later they were sorry not to have done so, though if it is any consolation to them, they were not the only ones who would come to regret their decision.

We entered into tough negotiations with Kuzbassrazrezugol, a coal-mining company owned by two well-known entrepreneurs: Mr Bokarev and Mr Makhmudov. This was no one-day talk – it dragged on and on, across a number of meetings, with both sides arguing fiercely, seemingly unwilling to give even an inch. Eventually, we were able to persuade them that the long-term strategic benefits of operating this terminal far outweighed the costs of the initial investment, though even once we'd reached an agreement between the state and Kuzbassrazrezugol, the complex ownership structure and status had to be resolved. Finally, however, we settled all these questions, they paid the considerable sum of $4 million, and we set to work on building Russia's most modern coal terminal.

The involvement of Mr Bokarev and Mr Makhmudov, who had previously owned shares in the port at Tallinn, was an important symbol of our progress – and the very existence of the coal terminal gave us something tangible we could show to convince other potential investors – but this was not in itself sufficient to outweigh the challenges posed by a number of significant obstacles in our path – everything from a much-loved local fish to huge global institutions.

Take a map, look where St Petersburg is; you will see that the Finnish port of Kotka is almost next door. And just across the Gulf of Finland is Tallinn. Russian goods passing through their ports provided almost 10 per cent of their GDP. If they could stop Ust-Luga, they could protect their interests for decades to come – so we were hit at every level. On the one hand there was a subsidised campaign that was intended to demonstrate how the construction of the ports would ruin the ecology of the Gulf of Finland and the Baltic Sea – for instance, there was a ferocious attempt to highlight the danger it was alleged the development would pose to a special saltwater fish called the Koryushka (or smelt), which came to the region every year to breed in its marshes. The people of St Petersburg have a sentimental attachment to the Koryushka – during the spring it pervades the whole area with the smell of fresh cucumber – and now they were being told that it was likely that the port of Ust-Luga would destroy its habitat for ever.

There was also substantial resistance externally from institutions like the World Bank, who refused to support the Ust-Luga project, arguing that because Russia could use the Baltic ports, it should not develop its own (I was told this personally by someone from the World Bank). This was at the same time as our rivals were receiving political and financial support from the West. In 1998, the Baltic states and the US signed a document called the 'US–Baltic Charter', a significant statement of intent which committed Estonia, Latvia and Lithuania to supporting the work and values of the big Western international institutions such as the WTO, NATO and the EU. It was a decisive turn away from Russia, and a sign that the relationships that had once sustained the Warsaw Pact had been reduced to nothing more than a memory.

But, perhaps just as severely, there was huge internal opposition. In the years in which Russia did not possess its own port infrastructure in its north-west, it was inevitable that the export-ers would seek a relationship with Baltic states. And to them, unsurprisingly, the development at Ust-Luga represented a threat. After all, huge volumes of Russian oil were being shipped through the Baltic ports, at Tallinn more than any other com-modity. A company like Global Ports Investments PLC, which owned an oil terminal at the Muuga port in Tallinn, and whose major clients were Russian oil companies, had much to lose. As did Gunvor, the huge oil trading company that had interests in Tallinn, and Kinex, one of Russia's first privately owned oil trading companies, that held 50 per cent of the shares in the Sil-lamäe port in Estonia. These were huge enterprises, with massive resources, which could exert a real sway – imagine the influence that companies such as BP or Shell could bring to bear if they wanted to obstruct a project that conflicted with their interests. Formal lobbying of government officials was accompanied by carefully worded phrases delivered into the ears of those close to the levers of power, and a concerted campaign in the press ('Why bother with this white elephant when we already can use the Baltic ports? It's a waste of time and money!' 'They're crooks! If you give them any kind of support, that cash will vanish; we'll never see it again.')

Perhaps if after Boris Yeltsin had made his declaration regard-ing the foundation of Ust-Luga in 1993 he and the government he led had actually buttressed it with decisive policies, or even just made it clear publicly that they supported the project, then things would have been different. But the ambiguous messages that emerged from the Kremlin failed to make it clear that there was outright support, which gave many licence to ignore or

obstruct our work. (Though given the adverse economic conditions, and the fact that as much as half of the orders that emerged
from the Kremlin at the time were being ignored, an argument
could be made that there was little even someone with a strong
desire to help us could have done.) One concrete step that
Moscow could have taken – but always shied away from – was
the introduction of punitive tariffs to encourage Russian carriers
to send their cargo through Ust-Luga. It would have made our
progress immeasurably faster. Even when President Putin came
to power, some in his close circle lobbied against the idea. But
if he did not introduce the tariffs we were looking for, Mr Putin
was supportive in many other ways, not least by communicating
clearly that the Kremlin stood firmly behind Ust-Luga. In 2001,
during one particularly critical phase in the port's development,
he called a government meeting where he announced that the
work at Primorsk, Ust-Luga and other port developments was
being sabotaged and that the 'saboteurs are sitting in this very
room'. Things changed substantially after this intervention.

I remember vividly how in 2006 Mr Putin came to the port
for the first time to take a look at the progress of the project. By
this point I had joined Russian Railways, but because of my long
history with the project, and also the existence of a substantial
rail development at the port, I had insisted he should come because I wanted him to see with his own eyes what we had built.
After all, it was at the time the sole major infrastructure project
in the whole country to be anywhere close to fulfilment. We
looked together at the fully operational terminals and I showed
him the ones that catered for the super-cargo ships; I talked him
through the plans we had to introduce fully automated sorting

stations (which remain the only ones in existence in Russia), and then, as I escorted him to his helicopter, he turned to me and told me that he was both surprised and pleased. He said that some of the men around him had told him it would be a mistake to go because all he would see would be empty fields, at best a degraded Potemkin village; that it would be a disgrace for the President to be associated with it. But now I could tell from his body language that he was not just surprised, he was proud.

Putin's visit was a big statement of political intent. It encouraged those bureaucrats who had previously been dragging their feet to take it more seriously and was a clear sign to businessmen of the direction in which government policy was heading. I knew there had been a decisive change in the atmosphere when a good friend, who was the owner of one of the firms who had previously invested heavily in a terminal at Tallinn, came to me to complain about a reprimand he had received from his wife. He had been running his mouth off about Ust-Luga and the trouble he claimed it was causing him when his wife suddenly interrupted him. 'You're a traitor,' she told him. 'You don't think about the interests of your country, you think only about your bottom line. Mr Yakunin has the right idea; he's doing the correct thing!' I could not help but smile as the owner told me that since I was ruining his family life, he would need to change his attitude to my project.

Businessmen are clever people and they do not operate in a vacuum – their livelihood depends on more than just the numbers on their spreadsheets. If the mood of the authorities changes, then so do the plans of tycoons. And when the oil-trading behemoth Gunvor made the decision to build a terminal at Ust-Luga in preference to other ports, we realised that the tide had turned. That such a big company, which was effectively created in Tallinn and had such close links to the Baltic ports, had chosen to invest in our development was a hugely significant indication of our success.

From that point on, progress accelerated rapidly. In less than a decade the cargo turnover at Ust-Luga grew from 0.8 million tonnes to almost 80 million tonnes. At the beginning of the development, we had only dreamt of handling 30 million tonnes of cargo, but now it is easy to see how it would be possible to develop the port to 100 million, or even 120 million tonnes. No other Russian port in the Baltic has seen such growth. In 2008, Ust-Luga's share of the freight volume passing through Russia's Baltic ports was 9 per cent; by 2013, that figure had risen to 78 per cent. There are eleven terminals currently operating in the port, including ones for coal, general cargo, sulphur, containers, timber and oil. It is already one of the biggest ports in Europe and the second-largest in the Baltic Sea (and handles as much cargo as the rest of the Baltic ports added together), and it is going to be, possibly, if not the largest, definitely one of the two largest ports in Europe.

It is hard now not to be reminded of a comment Mr Izrailit made when he first came to look at the site of the project he had taken on. 'We arrived there and it was like the Tunguska meteorite had landed: trees felled, land turned upside down, a mound of sand leaking into the bay, and some miserable-looking swans swimming nearby.' We had talked during the project's earliest days about how we could make Ust-Luga into another Amsterdam or Rotterdam; it had seemed almost like a joke. That the management of the port of Tallinn, our main competitor, sent us a telegram of congratulations after our own project's opening ceremony was a sign that our efforts were being taken seriously. And nobody would laugh at our founding ambitions now.

By 1998, reformers from both within and without the country had been urging red-blooded capitalism on Russia for years. They believed that if we introduced a layer of owners into the top of society then everything would change: wealth would trickle down, enriching us all. It was an illusion, based on the false premise that the same medicine can be administered to patients suffering from different ailments (and look what eminent economists like Joseph Stiglitz are saying now – perhaps neo-liberalism was not even the answer in the West). They knew everything there was to know about the free-market economy, but in truth they knew nothing about the situation in Russia. Sometimes I wonder what they think about it now. Do they look at the destruction and chaos they left in their wake and feel regret?

The PPP arrangement we introduced felt as if it illuminated a different path for Russia to follow; one that showed that the state still had a role as a major actor, whether or not it was collaborating with private interests. Instead of constantly pleading for help from the West, we could find another way to build our economy through developments such as Ust-Luga, and, despite substantial internal and external opposition, we could also remind our country of the extent to which its infrastructure is also its backbone.

CHAPTER FIVE

HOW TO WIN FRIENDS AND INFLUENCE PEOPLE

You do not always realise during the course of your first encounter with someone the role they might go on to play in your life. Hindsight is a wonderful thing, though sometimes I wish it did not wait so long before revealing its wisdom.

Though we had both served in the secret services, I did not meet Vladimir Putin properly until 1992, in St Petersburg, although I was familiar with his name; it is a small enough city that you soon hear about anyone of interest. We met when I was involved in a number of projects designed to attract investment into the region. We knew that support from the local government would be crucial, and to this end arranged a meeting at the office of the deputy mayor (as he was then), where we talked him through a new business venture that I was contemplating together with a number of partners. Time went by, we managed to persuade investors to put money up to boost the city's development, and we gave little more thought to the quiet, attentive man who had seemed somewhat interested in our proposals.

It was not until the aftermath of the constitutional crisis of 1993, when President Yeltsin's dispute with the Duma ended with tanks shelling the White House, that we thought of contacting Putin again. With the Communist Party now completely prohibited, it became clear to us that the outlawed organisation owned, or perhaps I should say controlled, a great deal of property (after all, the concept of private ownership had not really existed in the Soviet Union), and that the mayor's office might be interested in selling it for the benefit of the city. Since we had contacts on both sides then, we realised we might be the best people to arrange this joint venture.

Which is how we found ourselves in Mr Putin's company once more. I have known him for a long time now, and am alive to his many qualities, but I do not think that either of us, as we sat in his office all those years ago, could have imagined the future that lay before us, or, indeed, our country. For the avoidance of doubt it is perhaps worth me saying this here: since Vladimir Putin became President in 2000, I believe that his achievements include preventing the disintegration of the Russian Federation, establishing a stable political system, introducing a clear administrative structure, and reformulating the relationship between business and the state. Under his leadership, a number of major infrastructure projects have been completed, something that I believe has made an important contribution to the nation's wellbeing. I supported too his attempts at the beginning of his time in office to strengthen relationships with the West. But I am certainly not someone who has cheered everything he has done – I do not agree, for instance, with the economic policies that his government has pursued and is still pursuing, notably the prioritisation of social and other current budget expenses over capital investments, and the allocation of the nation's foreign reserves. My opinion is that pursuing a course of pure monetarism is not sufficient to meet the demands of restoring an economy still reeling from the brutal blow it suffered during the first years of perestroika. But I am getting ahead of myself.

Perhaps we had all hoped for too much in the immediate aftermath of the Soviet Union's collapse. It now seems barely conceivable that anyone could have believed in the possibility of creating a healthy, functioning, market-orientated society out of the rubble of the Soviet Union. Britain has a long experience of parliamentary rule, one that has evolved gradually over many centuries and which is embodied in many institutions and traditions that extend well beyond Westminster itself – but in 1991, our people did not even have a picture in their head of how a democracy really worked. A disproportionate share of the nation's economy, as well as almost the entirety of its media, was controlled by a handful of apparatchiks, remnants of the old system whose presence reminded us how little had really changed. There is more to a democracy, we learned during these years, than simply holding elections. The right to vote means very little when your business is seized from you by criminals, or yet another financial collapse sees your savings disappear overnight.

It is still stranger to remember that there was a time when Boris Yeltsin had been the most popular figure in the country, the only politician who many of the population had ever trusted. But all of this goodwill had been squandered by the end of the millennium.

The ailing President alternated between bouts of incoherent disorientation and periods of withdrawal that might easily have been mistaken for depression. He had suffered several heart attacks already even before the 1996 election, and there were whispers too that his drinking habit had corroded his mind – but what caused his weakness was perhaps less important than the fact that it left a black hole at the centre of government, one which frustrated any attempt to inject the administration with energy or direction. It was a drifting, aimless husk of a presidency whose very emptiness threatened the country Yeltsin was supposed to be safeguarding. There were odd moments, increasingly rare ones, when he would still be animated by a lightning bolt of enthusiasm, recovering for a couple of days his old flamboyance and energy, his capacity to pull political solutions from the ether, the atomic fizz of his charisma. They were long enough to prompt a half-blink of hope within his circle, and yet even they would soon be disappointed again.

The surprise appointments that he had once used to wrong-foot opponents and allies alike no longer had the galvanising impact of times past. He was a senile magician, confusedly casting old spells that had long since lost their power. Prime ministers would be sacked and then reappointed six months later. He brought in young tyros and weather-bitten veterans, but none seemed able to make the difference our country so desperately needed. The only lasting effect of his fickleness was the alienation of an entire generation of experienced bureaucrats and politicians, a process that left Yeltsin exposed and lonely, and overly reliant on a tiny inner circle that soon became known as 'the Family'. This group included at various times his daughter, Tatyana; Tatyana's husband,

Valentin Yumashev, who afterwards became the head of the presidential administration; Oleg Deripaska (who was married to Yumashev's daughter from his first marriage); the chief of staff, Alexander Voloshin; the head of security Alexander Korzhakov; Anatoly Chubais; and the oligarchs Boris Berezovsky (who had not yet discovered the enthusiasm for democratic accountability that he would be so vocal about in later years) and Roman Abramovich.[10] They insulated the President, but in the process created an airless, suffocating atmosphere that cut him off from reality. He was no longer able to speak to, or understand, the annihilating lack of hope felt by the majority of his subjects. That many houses had televisions now meant little; their inhabitants had lost almost everything else.

Yeltsin had always been fond of grand gestures, but it was only after we had become acquainted with their consequences that we realised how dangerous this could be. In 1990 he had cheerfully encouraged Russia's federal subjects 'to take as much sovereignty as you can swallow'. Maybe he did not think his audience would take him seriously, or perhaps he simply did not understand what the likely repercussions of his statement might be (like Gorbachev, he was in favour of national expression, but appalled by the idea of secession). His words were followed almost immediately by a flourish of ethnic violence, the rise of a number of extreme nationalist movements, and even the return of a number of ghosts from the past, with fevered talk of the creation of a Siberian Republic. Chechnya declared independence

---

10 If you are interested in how these people operated, and the principles of the world they inhabited, the transcripts of the case Berezovsky tried to bring against Abramovich in the London courts several years later make highly informative reading.

unilaterally the following year and saw its economy turned over to racketeers, and its morality entrusted into the hands of Islamic radicals. Their demands were echoed by many of the other republics, such as Tatarstan and Bashkortostan, gathered along Russia's south-eastern fringe.[11] Though the December 1993 constitution took the first steps towards establishing federalism, the country's weakness and volatility mean that Moscow's grasp over its subjects was slipping.

Governors began to openly defy the federal state as provincial political and economic elites collaborated with gangs of bandits to enrich themselves on a grand scale. Government money was ruthlessly expropriated and those who had come to try and reclaim it were sent back to Yeltsin with their tails between their legs. Many regional legislatures adopted laws declaring sovereignty. They asserted ownership over natural resources, laid claim to the airspace above their territory and even began to start conducting foreign policies independent of Moscow.

The inevitable offensive launched in Chechnya in 1994 was as badly conceived and ill thought through as the policies that had preceded it and was soon attended by catastrophe. It seemed that even when Yeltsin tried to preserve the country's fragile integrity, his every clumsy swipe only made it weaker. As the '90s wore on, the idea that the collapse of the Soviet Union might be followed

---

11 The Soviet Union had been made up of fifteen national republics (Russia, Ukraine, Belarus, Estonia, Latvia, Lithuania, Uzbekistan, Kazakhstan, Moldova, Tajikistan, Georgia, Armenia, Turkmenistan, Azerbaijan and Kyrgyzstan). In theory, each republic had equal status within the arrangement, but in practice it was dominated by Moscow (interestingly, the only republic without its own Communist Party was Russia). For most of its existence Russia (formally, the Russian Socialist Federative Republic) itself contained seventeen autonomous republics, some of which, after the dissolution of the Soviet Union and the formation of the Russian Federation, could not understand why they too had not been given independence. Republics like Tatarstan, for instance, pointed to territory the size of Texas and the fact that it contributed as much as 20 per cent of the country's GDP.

by the disintegration of Russia itself ceased to be only a nightmare and became instead a disturbingly plausible possibility.

Before long, the violence that had become such a feature of life on Russia's periphery found its way to the country's centre. Politicians were shot in the stairway of their homes, the blood spreading from their still-warm bodies just another stain on the dismal body politic. I still remember vividly the assassination in St Petersburg of the vice governor Mikhail Manevich, who was gunned down on his way to work in August 1997. As I stood at the memorial service alongside Mr Chubais and a number of the other men who figured in the city's political life, such as Alexei Kudrin and Herman Gref (I would encounter many of them again when I moved to Moscow), as well as the massed ranks of the city's officials, and people from every echelon of St Petersburg society, an air of disbelief – that this kind, gentle man had been given a gangster's death – reigned. In the weeks that followed, there was a rapid expansion of the personal security market. Soon it was no longer unusual to see black-clad men wielding Kalashnikovs guarding the entrances to the city's restaurants.[12]

The President's reckless attempts over the years to fold the fledgling democracy into his personality – so that to many they were almost one and the same – meant that the government's struggles were ascribed to his own failings. There had been a time when the

---

12 Despite its viciousness, perhaps *because* of it, this violence eventually petered out. This was partly because many of those criminals involved slipped into business suits and involved themselves in legitimate activity, but mostly because after five years there was nobody left to kill. The most prominent protagonists were either dead or had fled abroad. It was a tragic state of affairs that eventually consumed itself.

sight of enemies circling would have been a source of energy, a sign that he was moving in the right direction. By 1999, however, he was increasingly trapped, wracked by thoughts about how he, his family and his circle might survive after his resignation. If it had been 1994, or even 1996, he might have been able to channel his populist gift and summon some kind of escape; a deal could have been struck and catastrophe averted. As it was, 'the Family' began to search frantically for a successor who they could trust to protect them. They knew their history, and did not need to be told how vulnerable those who have recently lost power quickly become. Soon, they settled upon the director of the FSB, a former KGB lieutenant colonel from St Petersburg called Vladimir Putin.

Vladimir Putin was not born a president. At the time of his elevation he was still, despite his time as head of the FSB and the President's Chief Control Directorate, someone with a reputation as a local politician. Though St Petersburg is Russia's second city, few major politicians have emerged from it since the wild days of the 1917 revolution. It was very rare, during the Soviet era, that anyone from St Petersburg was brought into the highest echelons of power – the city's proximity to the West, its democratic traditions, its assertive intelligentsia and persistent appetite for freedom, all served to make its residents suspect in the eyes of the Communist Party apparatus. But Putin had one significant feature that marked him out from almost all of his contemporaries: he kept his word. This, as much as anything, recommended him to 'the Family'.

The Russian people were undoubtedly ready for a man like Putin – he looked a different type of leader from Yeltsin. But

Putin's presidency also depended on the kingmakers around Yeltsin. They had seen the loyalty he had shown to his boss Anatoly Sobchak, the mayor of St Petersburg; Putin had stood shoulder to shoulder with the guards protecting Sobchak's office during the failed coup of 1991, and had remained loyal after he was deposed as mayor in 1996. They were confident they were bringing to power a man who never broke his promises – a quality without which Putin might not have become President, or at least not so soon.

There were other things about him they approved of too. His very obscurity, his ostensible lack of political ambition – he was, to begin with, incredibly reluctant to accept their proposal to lead the country, for he knew the price one pays, the life one loses, for taking on such a role – meant that he seemed to them a tabula rasa onto which they could inscribe their own agendas. Men like Berezovsky, who pushed hard for his appointment, were keenly excited by the prospect of installing another puppet in the government, the rest of 'The Family' looked forward to an untroubled future, and the only dissenting voice within the Yeltsin inner circle was the arch-moderniser Chubais, who would later admit he was wary of Putin's past.

But if Chubais feared that the new president would be a revanchist who would interrupt the liberalising reforms that had been initiated, with mixed results, during Yeltsin's reign, then his concerns would soon be assuaged.

Putin's political education had come at the hands of men like the liberal Sobchak. If his first life might be said to have been lived in the KGB, his second was in the crucible of St Petersburg politics during the '90s. He believed as strongly as his mentor in the urgent need to transform the fortunes of Russia's sick economy – and once he became President he continued the economic policies that had been initiated by his predecessor's government. (He had in fact agreed with the Family that he would not abandon the reforms they had begun.) If, for instance, you were to revisit his 2000 address to the Federal Assembly, you would see how much attention he devoted to fiscal issues. And given the strength of the neo-Communist faction in the Duma at the time, this was essential. Neither the people nor the country's elite wanted the apparatchiks to regain their grip on power. What reforms had been achieved since 1991 still rested on fragile foundations, and turning the clock back would erode them entirely (however, even this attitude was occasionally bent out of shape by contradictions – for example, by the early 2000s, only a minority of the population opposed the renationalisation of state assets).

Putin's faith in liberalism was complemented by experiences and qualities that set him apart from his contemporaries, whether at home or abroad. Perhaps the most notable difference is that he served for many years in the KGB, a fact that has been the source of endless specious speculation. (George H. W. Bush was another national leader in recent history with a secret-service background – he was briefly the director of the CIA – but I cannot help but note that nobody ascribes the same importance to this as they do to Putin's time in the KGB.)

There are things one learns in the secret services that are taught in few other trades. Some are very specific: for example, you are given the psychological tools to help you understand the motives of other people, to the point that sometimes you are able to divine things about your subject that he does not know himself. I do not pretend to know the contents of Vladimir Putin's thoughts; I have, after all, been privy to only a small proportion of his conversations. But there are times when it has been clear to me as a spectator that he has used his ability to negotiate, persuade and cajole in order to achieve the result he wants. Perhaps the most notable example of this would be the way that he turned Akhmad Kadyrov, the Chechen commander who for years had been one of Russia's staunchest enemies, into an ally. When, finally, Kadyrov was detained, Vladimir Putin wasted no time in arranging a meeting. Nobody knows, least of all me, what kind of a talk they had, but he obviously found the right words to earn his trust and establish a foundation of mutual respect. Before long, a war that had once threatened to drag on for years had come to an end.

Another aspect of the education one receives in the secret services is harder to articulate, since it bears little relation to any other discipline. There is only one rule: when you are presented with an order you must follow it; you do not have the right to challenge what you are being asked to do. And few people ask any questions as long as you achieve your targets. Perhaps this can be best summed up by a popular Russian saying: 'Winners cannot be prosecuted.' (Though, increasingly nowadays, I have noticed that people are more interested in means than they are ends.)

It is a mindset evolved for coping with extremity, and yet much about it – full-blooded devotion to a cause, an unflinching sense of duty and self-sacrifice, and an adamantine singleness of purpose, among others – might easily be seen to have a place in politics too. Not that this type of experience is without its own drawbacks.

Lucky is the man who, in the course of this work, has not been involved in something – whether as a protagonist or only a witness, whether deliberate or accidental – that cripples for ever their human nature. Vladimir Putin is, I believe, one of those fortunate few that have managed to survive with their conscience intact.

(It is extremely rare for civilians to ever find themselves exposed to such potentially compromising circumstances, but in the dark years in which their country was demolished, years in which ordinary people found themselves in situations more brutal and distressing than they could ever have imagined, almost everybody in Russia has done something that one could judge as immoral.)

Putin also benefited from the fact that although he was seen by many as embodying some of the best features of the old regime, because he had been an agent working in the GDR rather than a politician operating in Moscow, he was not tainted with its failures.

So while Putin's appointment was initially greeted with surprise – few outside his home city knew much of him – for the first time in years it seemed as if there was a reason to feel positive about the future of Russia. Not, of course, that this optimism blinded anyone to the gravity of the nation's situation as it entered a new millennium.

The questions that had plagued the end days of Yeltsin's administration had not gone away just because a new face was sitting in the Kremlin. Would Russia as we knew it continue to even exist? Would it remain a plaything of the oligarchs? How could the rule of law be re-established and power consolidated? What could be done to transform an ailing economy? It was an awkward, tense time. One wrong step could see the President tumbling out of power or, worse, could lead to violence on the streets.

Though in large part Putin left the management of the economy to his finance and economic ministers, Kudrin and Gref, who were encouraged to continue with privatisation and liberalising reforms, steadily the administration of the country began to be structured differently. In quick succession, measures were introduced to crack down on tax evasion, and to provide state funding for political parties so that they could no longer act as vehicles for billionaires' resentments and ambitions. The extension of private land ownership was followed by the establishment of a judicial system based on the Napoleonic Code. A civil code and laws on arbitration courts were introduced, the status of judges was approved and the courts themselves were strengthened.

These were all small steps in themselves, but each was vital, and each was a reminder that any progress the country was making in the right direction was the result of enormous collective effort by a number of politicians. I sometimes get the sense that people outside Russia think that our president enjoys unlimited power. But it is not possible for just one man by himself to turn a country upside down; even the tsars did not enjoy this kind of undiluted, omnipotent influence. (Though, in my opinion, President Putin does possess a gift for making decisions, which I believe is one of the hallmarks of a strong leader.)

It was clear too from the beginning that this was not a programme that could be implemented overnight. Nor, in fact, was it a programme that could be implemented fully within a year. It is easy to transform a small country of 1.5 million people like

Estonia in a comparatively short space of time, but reforming a colossus like Russia is an entirely different proposition. I do not think it is surprising that, eighteen years later, there still remains much to be done.

One of the new President's most significant achievements in his first years in the Kremlin was to arrest the ascendancy of the oligarchs, a group of fabulously rich power-brokers who, during the '90s, had come to play an outsized role in the nation's political and economic life. While in 1996 Yeltsin had only been able to win the election by handing over huge chunks of state assets to these men in exchange for their support, in 2000, Vladimir Putin was confirmed as Russia's leader, winning a majority with almost no campaigning. It was in the face of this surge of popular excitement that these wealthy corrupt men realised, too late, that they had endorsed a politician who threatened their pre-eminence. Over the past decade, each of these men had accumulated titanic wealth and influence. They had come to believe that there was little left to stop them turning Russia into something approaching a personal fiefdom, so as soon as it became clear that Russia had elected a president willing not only to defy them, but to actually challenge the foundations of their hegemony, they realised that they would have to try to fight back.

They had thrived in the immoral economy that had reigned since the dissolution of the Soviet Union, where power and people could be bought as if they were toys, and children aspired to be bandits and hard-currency prostitutes.[13] Between 1996 and 2000,

---

13 A hard-currency prostitute, or *interdevochka* in Russian (literally international girl), is a prostitute who works for convertible foreign currency, selling sex mostly to foreigners.

the group of oligarchs known as the *Semibankirschina* (the seven bankers) possessed a significant proportion of Russia's finances. Before I became CEO of Russian Railways, I commissioned a special piece of research into the Russian economic landscape. It told me that 46 per cent of the nation's economy was concentrated in the hands of just eight families, and that within four years, if nothing was done to stop them, this figure would reach 51 per cent. These businessmen had used their immense riches – seized in the main during the scandalous privatisations of the previous decade – to buy newspaper and television channels, as well as huge influence in the Duma, where sitting politicians were bribed and puppet candidates pushed forward. Boris Berezovsky, who in the first few months of 2000 was telling anyone willing to listen that it was he who had brought Putin into power, had once said that 'Russian politics is a modern version of Russian roulette'. He and his associates had spun the chamber too many times to count and had always got lucky, but things were going to be different now.

It helped that Putin realised quickly something that the oligarchs only understood very dimly themselves: they were despised. The Russian people hated the oligarchs' flaunting of their colossal riches – the private planes, the super-yachts, the sprawling villas on the French Riviera, and the way this ostentation was combined with a supreme disregard for the wellbeing of the millions of their countrymen. By contrast, Putin's stern, ascetic demeanour, the fact that he had been seen to refuse many of the luxuries and blandishments on offer to those in power, indicated to many that he was the man to save the nation that had become a land lost to hope.

The first sign that the winds had changed direction came before the presidential election of 2000, when one of the oligarchs swaggered into Putin's office, making the same visit he always paid to new candidates. The oligarch wanted to make it clear to the politician before him that he stood no chance of winning any election without the support he and his fellow businessmen could offer. What kind of deal, he enquired, did Putin intend to make with them? I do not think that the oligarch expected the substance of the reply he received, or the tone in which it was delivered.

This was followed by a televised meeting in July 2000, where the President summoned twenty-five of the most prominent members of Russia's business elite to the Kremlin to tell them that their attempts to dominate the government's agenda would no longer be tolerated. It was a profound and long-overdue realignment in the relationship between capital and state power.

I remember speaking in 2013 with a professional acquaintance, who might be classed as an oligarch, a number of years after Berezovsky and Gusinsky had been expelled, and Khodorkovsky imprisoned. I was talking to him about how some of the government's decisions around this time might be seen to have been prejudicial to the success of private businessmen like him. 'Yes,' he told me, 'I hated it.' When I asked him why he had stayed silent while his business was effectively under attack, he replied that 'In 2004 we were given a clear signal not to intervene in politics, and that was enough.'

Vladimir Putin had inherited a barely functioning quasi-market economy that was built in many places on a rotten foundation of criminality. But although the budget was empty, inflation rampant, and the education and health systems devastated, the new President was alive to the importance of thinking strategically about the Russian economy. He knew that there were no short-term solutions to long-term afflictions and threw his weight behind a programme of infrastructure investment and development that was essential if the country were to be able to compete on the global stage in the years to come. As deputy Minister of Transport, I was involved with the construction of the ports of Primorsk and Ust-Luga – projects that had been initiated but not completed during Yeltsin's time in power – and I saw at first hand the impact Putin's courage and force had on their success. He identified himself unbelievably closely with these transformative but highly controversial endeavours. Had any of them failed, it would have been a tremendous, perhaps even fatal, blow to his reputation.

It would, however, be a mistake to regard these efforts as some kind of outlier. Rather, the work conducted by the Transport Ministry between 2000 and 2002, and the challenges we faced, might be seen in some respects as a case study of what was happening elsewhere across the country.

We were dealing with a sector of the economy that was only partially reformed, with some areas completely privatised, others little changed from their Soviet incarnations. Furthermore, the transport sector had been hit hard by the dissolution of the USSR, which had deprived it of many of the ports, ships and other key elements upon which it had depended prior to 1991. The system as a whole was threatening to degenerate into an incoherent mess, something that would have profound consequences for the economy. The fate of the components of the internal waterways system, which had been almost completely privatised, showed us clearly what would happen if we did not take action fast. Because there had been no central coordination, and no private company willing to undertake the unprofitable tasks of maintenance, the rivers soon silted up and the fleet was allowed to degrade. Russia had been deprived of an important method of transport and communication, and this loss had its own unfortunate consequences. For instance, since barely any cargo was being ferried along the rivers, the demand for river-going boats fell abruptly, and so the shipyards that had previously been busy sites of construction and maintenance no longer had much reason to exist.

But even without these issues, the collapse of central authority under the previous administration meant that in many parts of Russia, even once we had created a defined transport strategy, it was a struggle to secure the support we needed from the powerful regional governors. However sincere our intentions, however well considered our plans, however high the stakes, there was no guarantee we would succeed.

My appearance in Moscow in 2000, where as deputy minister at the Transport Ministry I was charged with particular responsibility for port development, international cooperation and the coordination of different transport development and investment programmes (most notably with the railways), had been almost accidental. One of Vladimir Putin's first actions after he came to power was to rationalise the country's unwieldy administrative architecture, and my role at the North-West Inspectorate of the Chief Control Department of the President, as well as the jobs of my twenty-one fellow inspectors, were victims of this. Because our work and responsibilities overlapped fairly substantially with the activities of those people who reported directly to the President, it was decided to make the once independent regional inspectorates answerable directly to the office of the President's Representatives in the Regions.

In the meantime, however, Sergei Frank, the Minister of Transport, who I had worked with closely on a number of port projects already, invited me to work with him. The first Putin knew of the move was when Mr Frank informed him of his plan for my appointment. (I later learned that the President had told his transport minister that there were two things he needed to know about me: first that I was a tough, straight-talking guy, so much so that I could talk my way into trouble, and second that I could be trusted to do whatever task was set before me.)

But nobody seems interested in this kind of Russian story – a complex one of technocratic happenchance. Most people assume – perhaps it would be more accurate to say that people prefer to believe – a tale riddled with conspiracy: that I was part of the cabal of former KGB operatives infiltrated into the Russian government by a President determined to fight the cold war all over again; that at Ozero, the dacha cooperative in which I was once, long ago now, involved with Putin (he left the group many years ago), we plotted how we could divide the country's riches among ourselves. That there is no truth in these suggestions, or what truth there is has been distorted and twisted beyond recognition, does not bother them; they only want to hear accounts that confirm the prejudices they already hold about Russia.

Ultimately, Putin was responsible for my relocation to the

capital, but only indirectly. It was not because he parachuted the men with whom he had once shared a holiday home into responsible positions, but because of his interest in reforming every element of Russia's bureaucratic system, which had the unplanned consequence of making my old role redundant, and ensured that I had to look for new opportunities.

Putin's restructuring of the way that power flowed around the country was one of his most significant early actions. He was not only interested in the commands themselves, he was also engaged, in a way that his predecessors had not been, with the way in which those commands were being implemented and how answerable or not the people charged with implementing them were to him. He understood how to make sure that if he signed something it would be put into effect not just in the square mile outside the Kremlin, but in the very far reaches of the country too.

As I watched this transformation of the way in which Russia was administrated, from my tiny new office in the Transport Ministry, I was trying to get used to a very different kind of existence to that to which I had been previously accustomed. Anyone who has lived all their life in St Petersburg will know the strangeness of coming to the capital from the periphery. In Moscow, even people from big cities are seen as provincial. This feeling of disorientation was exacerbated, to begin with at least, by the challenges posed by getting to grips with an unfamiliar role.

At the time, Sergei Frank was one of the few ministers who thought strategically. He taught me that the state should have an integrated plan for development that included every element of the transport system, rather than treating railways and ports as separate spheres. It was also the strong belief of Sergei Frank that the Transport Ministry he headed should be a dynamic one – initiating projects instead of simply responding to events. Rather than working in a piecemeal fashion, his vision was that everything we did should be in accordance with a strategic plan that, once implemented, would harness the considerable latent potential of our transport infrastructure and put it at the service of the country's economy.

One of the reasons why this potential remained latent, not realised, was that reform in this sector had hitherto been enacted in a notably inconsistent fashion. While the rail monopoly remained entirely in the state's hands, the ports had been sold off – so, for instance, there was no coherent system for getting a load of coal from a rail wagon to a cargo ship. JSC Novorossiysk Commercial Sea Port, the largest port operator in Russia, was already a partially privatised company in which the state owned only a minority of the shares, and JSC Ust-Luga a PPP enterprise. Privatisation had led in many instances to greater competition and efficiency, but Russia's economic resurgence depended on marrying these advances with a nationally implemented strategy and governmental oversight. The breaking apart of the monolithic Soviet transport system had created a fragmented situation in which the federal government, local authorities and private entrepreneurs rarely communicated, still less coordinated their operations. In the USSR, the same body had controlled both the airports and the planes that used them, but after 1991 the two operations were separated and left to fend for themselves in an environment without proper rules, regulations or legislation.

The transport system had become a fractured jumble of parts that moved independently of each other; what we were trying to do throughout the two years I spent at the Transport Ministry was to ensure as far as possible that they moved in concert. For example, we wanted to build, or modernise, ports that could each service the needs of a particular industry: Primorsk would carry oil, Ust-Luga would handle general cargo (including metals, coal, fertilisers, sulphur, machinery, ro-ro cargo, and a railway ferry), Vostochny would specialise in coal. Without a state-directed strategy, private enterprise would never even consider such an approach – why would they? Our role was to persuade them that not only would the country benefit if they were to get involved, but their businesses would thrive too.

You could compare us, I suppose, to an orchestra. No matter how talented the individual musicians are, no matter how beautiful the concert hall, if there is not a conductor they will only succeed in creating a discordant racket.

It was difficult, after having worked in the private sector and also the North-West Inspectorate, to find that, for all that some people continued to complain endlessly about government bureaucracy and red tape, at the heart of the system you actually had very little support. While there were several departments in the ministry who reported to me, I had no staff myself beyond a secretary and a single aide to help me do my job, and a suite of responsibilities that extended from the border with Finland to the Sea of Japan. And to begin with, I was unfamiliar with the relevant legislation, with the ministry's processes or even the key personalities within the transport system. It was precisely because I knew that I had large gaps in my knowledge that I set out to learn as much as I could about the mechanisms by which different elements in the country's transport infrastructure interacted, the importance of establishing connections between different industries, and, of course, the role that the Transport Ministry could play in all of this.

I had so much on my plate that I barely knew where to start, though my previous experience at Ust-Luga – where I had learned a great deal about port development and management as well as the way that they interacted with other elements within the transport system – gave me a good grounding in the area I was now working in. Many of the issues that I had encountered at Ust-Luga were reprised at the Transport Ministry – we were conscious of the absolute importance of reconciling public and private interests, but also the complexity and difficulty of doing so.

The other significant element was geo-political. Just as Ust-Luga was in part an attempt to redress the loss of the ports that had been assigned to the Baltic republics after the dissolution of the Soviet Union, so, for instance, at Novoship – the shipping company that operated out of Novorossiysk – we were trying to mitigate the consequences of the USSR's collapse on the country's cargo and passenger fleets. A large number of ships were given to Ukraine, with just a fragment remaining in our possession. If we wanted to rebuild the fleet to a standard that would make it competitive in the twenty-first century, then private investment was essential. Not least because foreign banks were unwilling to grant loans for ship construction and development to the Russian state (among other things, they were concerned about the stability of its banking system) and thus insisted that when Russian shipping companies wanted to place an order with foreign shipyards for a new ship, that a special new company should be created to be the owner of this ship and the bank's client.[14]

What this meant in practice was that each new ship was a separately constituted legal entity, and since there was no guarantee that their priorities would coincide with the Transport Ministry's strategic plan, this offered another potential hindrance to the kind of coordination we wished to achieve.

This problem was exacerbated by the fact that our sailors found themselves in a global economy, and under the influence of non-Russian institutions such as the foreign sailors' unions, who were attempting to persuade their Russian members to demand a higher salary – something that culminated in them detaining those ships whose crew were not paid the wages the union deemed acceptable. If the ship-owners were to cave in, then it would make it substantially harder for them to compete with their foreign rivals, especially since at the very same time our competitiveness was being compromised by the high tariffs being charged by the Russian ports' operators and pilots, who were mostly privatised and thus free from any state regulation. Our negotiations with the operators and pilots were always fraught. Their leaders claimed that every attempt we at the Ministry made to reach an agreement was in fact an infringement on their rights – they even went so far as to claim that we were trying to suppress their ability to conduct business.

All these problems were eventually settled. The state took

---

14 They would also have to fly the flag of another country – the Marshall Islands were always popular.

greater control of the ports and legislation was introduced for their development, which included a provision allowing the government to set some tariffs (since it had built the ports and was responsible for safety and security, it was its right to do so). It was a period of adjustment, rationalisation and experiment that anticipated much of what would be happening elsewhere in the country over the following years. It had been a decade since we had swapped a malfunctioning version of socialism for a malfunctioning version of capitalism, but it was increasingly clear to almost everyone in the country that it was high time that the state reclaimed a measure of control over the operation of the economy. In return, it would assume responsibility, in accordance with the country's laws, to foster favourable conditions (legislative, administrative and investment) for economic and social development, and establish an appropriate balance between public and private interests.

I was constantly on the move during the years I was at the ministry; it sometimes felt as if half my existence was spent 30,000 feet above Russia, on my way to another of the country's far-flung ports. Every visit would be made up of a constant round of meetings: with the port authorities, with the region's governor, with representatives from the local transport authority, with private entrepreneurs and potential investors. How efficient were the safety and signalling systems in a particular port? Were government funds being spent in the correct fashion? Was each port being developed in accordance with the strategic plans we had laid out? My aim was always to secure as comprehensive a picture as possible as to how these very different elements, all of which had very different priorities, interacted with one another, and to identify where any grit had somehow been introduced into the machinery, so to speak, in order to help extract it.

It was during these years that I came to really know Russia. I saw more of her terrain than I ever had before, more than most will ever see in a lifetime: from Murmansk hundreds of miles north of the Arctic Circle, to Taman on the Black Sea, through to Nakhodka, which perches opposite Japan and the two Koreas. But this period was also an exemplary education in the way Russia worked at every level, its complex administrative ecology. I came to understand something of the intricacies of its government; how, so far from Moscow that they might as well be on another continent, the administrations of Russia's most remote regions interacted with federal bodies; or the transformative impact transport infrastructure could have on towns that had previously been bereft of even basic medical care.

For decades, even those governors who had not tried to grab sovereignty away from the Kremlin had been accustomed to ruling their territories almost like feudal lords, so, perhaps unsurprisingly, it was sometimes hard to persuade them of the importance of supporting the coal industry when they were thousands of miles away from the nearest mine. They recoiled at any attempts to, as they saw it, undermine their authority over their fiefdoms. The withering away of the state's authority under Yeltsin left them almost totally unresponsive to orders from Moscow, which for years had lacked the money or even the will to impose its governance. So your chances of achieving anything during this period of time depended substantially on the nature of your relationship with them.

In the KGB (as in many other administrative or managerial organisations) we believed there were two main ways one could be persuasive. The first, perhaps the most straightforward, was to obtain some kind of compromising information about your subject that you could deploy to influence their behaviour. The second was to make them your friend (perhaps it will surprise you to learn that Dale Carnegie's *How to Win Friends and Influence People* was a key title on our syllabus). I had always favoured the second option – the bonds and obligations formed by that kind of relationship are far more durable and productive – and I built on the foundation I had established during my training when I encountered the friendly and open attitude displayed by the men and women I dealt with in New York, a city where it was never acceptable to use the word 'problem'.

I was lucky enough that I was never on the end of a brutal refusal by any of the governors, but then I was always aware of the need to prepare properly for these conversations, and approach them in the appropriate manner. I knew that it was not sufficient to talk about abstract state interests. Why should a governor in the west of the country care about supporting industrial development in its eastern extremities? You had to demonstrate in clear terms how whatever project you were talking about at the time would ultimately bring benefits to his region.

There were other, more direct, ways of securing regional support, as I learned later when I joined the Railways Ministry in 2002. As a huge ministry, we had considerable purchasing power. So if, for instance, a particular territory in which we wanted to create a project also contained a factory making the kinds of boots our workers needed to ensure their safety and comfort, it was always possible to reach a mutually beneficial agreement in which the contract for manufacturing the boots would be given to this region's factory (a contract big enough that it would help stimulate other elements of the local economy and provide ancillary social benefits too) in return for permission for us to implement another part of our national strategy.[15] The goodwill built up in the course of these exchanges meant that any future discussion would be all the easier and more productive.

As time went on, the administrative reforms enacted by Vladimir Putin began to erode some of the regions' ability to defy Moscow's authority. This culminated in December 2004 with the decision that the leaders of the Russian Federation's regions and republics would in the future be appointed by the President rather than elected, and that a number of the Federation's smaller units would be abolished. It was a decision attended by a huge deal of controversy and, in places, anger, but what has perhaps not been fully appreciated is the extent to which this centralisation of power was anticipated by the liberal finance minister Kudrin's sophisticated reforms of the financial system. Mr Kudrin introduced changes that meant that the Ministry of Finance alone had the power – which was unchecked – to provide the subventions and subsidies upon which the governors relied so heavily. As a result, the regions were left almost wholly at the mercy of the federal government's financial arm. Since the majority of the regions ran a more or less permanent debt (even today, only four or five are in profit) they were powerless to object. By the time the 2004 legislation was enacted, authority had already been de facto returned to the centre.

---

15 This took place before legislation that regulated the procurement of state-owned companies was introduced. Now they must buy goods and services in an open tender and auction process.

Nevertheless, it was a valuable reminder of the progress that had been made in just four years. Though a great deal of work lay ahead of the country, it was no longer on the verge of fragmentation or implosion, and the hold exerted over it by the oligarchs had been decisively broken – replaced with a new settlement in which it was acknowledged that the price these men would pay if they wanted to accumulate wealth was a complete withdrawal from the political arena. Much of the administrative apparatus of the country had been rationalised, something which would help provide a solid foundation for future economic growth, as would, of course, the work of the Transport Ministry.

I watched these later developments from the Railway Ministry. My role there was in many ways a continuation of the kind of work in which I had been involved under Sergei Frank, just focused on one particular element of the transport infrastructure. Leaving one ministry for another gave me the chance to reflect on everything that had taken place over the previous two years. Just as with the country as a whole, the scale of what we accomplished over the time I spent at the Transport Ministry was dwarfed by the scale of the work still to be done, but it still felt as if a corner had been turned. All around us, Russia was slowly being transformed, and we had played our part. It had felt, at the time, like a ceaseless round of conversation and persuasion played out in thousands of discussions that took place in every corner of the nation. These conversations are mostly forgotten now, their substance unrecoverable, but when I go, for instance, to the ports at Primorsk or Ust-Luga, St Petersburg, Vladivostok, Nachodka, Sochi, Taman, I can see how the countless arguments and consultations have been transformed into concrete achievements. Of that I am incredibly proud.

CHAPTER SIX

RUSSIAN REALITY

I had been an intelligence officer during some of the cold war's fiercest tensions, and in the years that followed I managed to carve out an existence in the midst of the chaotic free-for-all that was Russia during the '90s. I had been a high-ranking civil servant and had served as a deputy minister in two different government ministries, but I am not sure anything could have prepared me for this test: the biggest project and biggest challenge of my life – a period in which I had to learn so much complex new information that it was as if I had returned to university to take another degree.

Russian Railways had been charged with building the transport infrastructure that would be crucial if the 2014 Winter Olympics at Sochi were to go ahead. We were working to a fierce timetable in a location that you might think had been designed by God to obstruct the creation of railway lines, roads, bridges and tunnels. The project had been bedevilled by challenges from the very beginning, each of which we had overcome, and yet right then it was as if we'd run into a brick wall – or, more specifically, a mountain that lay on the north side of the Deep Yar Waterfall. Locals knew it as the Dragon's Mouth, which seemed somehow apt at that moment. The sub-contractors were supposed to be drilling through it what we had come to call Tunnel Complex No. 3 (there were six tunnel complexes in total), a stretch of combined road and railway over 3km long, but they could not lay their hands on the equipment necessary to make any progress through its complex mix of clay and limestone for another eight months. And even if they could get hold of the equipment sooner, they did not have sufficient capital to pay for it. The construction process had not even started, and already we had been confronted by a critical situation: unless we started drilling within the next month, there would be no way we would be able to complete this section of the route before the Olympics began. And the problems didn't end there. There were no accurate geological studies, and the structure of the mountain itself was so unusual that all the normal methods we had available to determine its architecture and composition were redundant.

If we could not find a way through this mass of rock, all our efforts so far would be wasted. I could not bear even to speculate as to what might have happened if we failed. I had spent a lifetime in the service of my country, had thrown every spare shred of energy I had into my role as CEO of Russian Railways, but if we were not able to deliver that transport infrastructure on time, it would be the end of my career – and perhaps even of the Olympics themselves. I am only half-joking when I say that I would probably have been encouraged to put a bullet in my own head. We could not afford to make the wrong decision. You can try to insulate yourself from failure by introducing into your organisation complex layers of oversight and analysis, but these take time to implement and will inevitably compromise your ability to act quickly and decisively. Nobody was going to turn around and say, 'Oh, don't worry, we know you were pressed for time, we know that you were faced by a thicket of insoluble challenges. Let's just forget about it.'

It would be humiliation on the grandest scale for the country, its people, its president and for me. There's an old Russian saying: 'Victory has many fathers but defeat has only one mother.' At Russian Railways, I was surrounded by an incredible team, including the Vice President Oleg Toni, who had particular responsibility for construction, but it would have to be me alone who took that decision, and me alone who answered for the consequences.

And the same question that weighed so heavily on me as I considered the problem in front of me – how do you go about drilling through a mountain when you do not know precisely what you'll find beneath its surface? – might reasonably have been reformulated to cover the whole Sochi enterprise: how do you successfully shepherd a megaproject to completion when the only thing you know for certain is that no plan survives contact with the real world?

One lesson that history seems determined to remind us of repeatedly is that Russian reality has always had a nasty habit of tripping up even the most elegant and plausible theories. The country is too big, too stubborn, too various, to ever submit itself fully to any kind of utopian scheme. The Bolsheviks, owners of a ferocious totalising impulse, discovered this, as did those who tried during the '90s to refashion the country as a paragon of free-market capitalism.

The Sochi Olympic Games were not, of course, designed to transform an entire society, but nonetheless grand hopes had been invested in them. By hosting the Games there – in this city which had, like much of the rest of the country, suffered a painful decline since the dissolution of the Soviet Union, but which was also afflicted by a host of problems that were very particular to it – there was a chance to develop a neglected region in Russia, to help promote Russia's image in the West, and to entice Russian tourists back from the ski slopes of Switzerland and France. It would also be a test of some of the seaworthiness of the economic reforms that had been introduced in the country – notably the reorganisations that Russian Railways had entered into.

In 2007, when the selection process began, there was an understanding among those people involved with running the economy that while Russia's financial position was steadily improving, the sheer number of tasks that still needed to be fulfilled, and the vast quantity of targets that still had to be reached if the country was to reverse decades of decline, imposed a brutal kind of realism on their planning. As a result, their priority was to concentrate their attention and resources on a single link in the chain that they could then drag out of the muck. If at that moment in time it was not possible to develop the economy as a whole, then far better to devote Russia's efforts in the most effective way and at the most effective point. And if investments were made into the creation of the infrastructure for that particular link, into its economy, into its education, which would encourage a whole range of other economic and social aspects to develop, then the belief was that the nation would see benefits elsewhere along the chain.

Another element in the government's thinking was that the people of Russia, buoyed by the fact that, for the first time in two decades, they were enjoying a sustained period of economic wellbeing, were beginning to travel all over the world, which meant that a lot of cash was leaving the country, and that, as a result, internal tourism was suffering. So one of the ideas was to use this Olympic Games programme as a way of establishing a place where Russians could feel comfortable going on holiday inside their own country.

But it was also designed to send a message to the rest of the world. Falling thirty-four years after the Moscow Olympics in 1980, it would be the first time the country had hosted a Summer or Winter Games since the end of the Soviet Union. Huge amounts of sentiment and national pride were invested in our ability to deliver something our country could be proud of and which would demonstrate the progress that had been made over the past decade.

Once the principle had been established, the obvious question was: where? There was no question that Sochi offered considerable scope for improvements. Indeed, previous bids for the Games, in 1998 and 2008, had been rejected by the International Olympic Committee, who cited the poor standard of the existing infrastructure to explain their decisions. By any metric you wanted to use, its infrastructure was either non-existent, or, at best, an antiquated hangover from the Soviet era. It was symptomatic of the asymmetric rate of progress in Russia. While large metropolises like Moscow and St Petersburg had been awash with money and influence since 1991 (even if it had often been shared unevenly), huge swathes of the country had been neglected, allowed to degrade. Because there was no industrial base in the region, there was no reliable supply of electricity, and the telephone and communications networks, sanitation, water supply and roads all fell drastically short of the demands of the twenty-first century. An incredible amount of work would be needed before it was anything like being fit for purpose.

The travel infrastructure was similarly deficient. For instance, the area's precipitous topography had ensured that there was no railway system that was even halfway capable of supporting an international event, and nor was there a highway connecting the resort to the rest of the country's road network – just a single B road, which threaded a precarious route between two high-altitude passes.

Furthermore, this once-beautiful stretch of coast, which during the Soviet Union had been one of the nation's most desirable tourist destinations, was suffering from profound environmental issues. Most of its raw sewage was being pumped directly into the sea. The stringent environmental regulations enforced by the Olympic Committee offered a notable opportunity to clean up this region's badly damaged ecology.

Tourist numbers had plummeted since the collapse of the Soviet Union. The end of communism made itself known in other ways too: several sanatoria closed down once the state subsidies for Sochi dried up and, following the disintegration of the multi-ethnic union, armed conflicts became an everyday reality in the Caucasus region. The civil war in Abkhazia, which flared up no more than 50km from the centre of Sochi, had devastated famous Soviet resort towns on the Black Sea Coast, such as Sukhumi.

Last but not least, there was one other unassailably significant reason for choosing Sochi: somewhat counterintuitively, the location and geography of this humid, Caucasian city meant that it was the best place in Russia to host a Winter Olympic Games. It cannot be too cold (no competitions can take place if the temperature falls below minus twenty degrees Celsius), which in February, when the Games would fall, excludes most territories in Russia. By contrast, Sochi is in the sub-tropics, which sounds like a problem, until you remember that, while the event is known as the Winter Olympics, more than 50 per cent of the medal pool is awarded in the events which don't actually require winter conditions (for instance, all the ice events are held on artificial ice, so you do not need arctic conditions).

The second, related, point concerns the kind of mountain present in the area, since these are integral to the alpine events. (What is not integral, contrary to what one might expect, is snow: while finding the right topographical profile is crucial, the pace of technological development has rendered natural snowfall unnecessary.) It has to be possible to create runs with a height difference of as much as 1,000m, and a height difference alone is insufficient; the slope must also be steep enough. Neither the Ural nor the Altai mountain ranges possessed the requisite height difference, and in European Russia, only the Caucasus (where Sochi was situated) and Khibiny (which regularly experiences temperatures in February of minus thirty) were steep enough. So while Russia is huge, there were no other locations in the country that satisfied all the Olympic Committee's requirements regarding topography and temperature.

All this meant that there was widespread support for the idea of hosting the Winter Games in Sochi. And when they were awarded to the city in July 2007, the news was celebrated as a national triumph.

Projects evolve into mega-projects when the scale increases, when the investment is huge and the complexity vast, when they have a long-lasting effect on a country's economy, society and environment. It was clear from the beginning that by any metric you wanted to use, Sochi was going to be one of the biggest mega-projects Russia had ever undertaken.

Once the decision had been made that the Olympic Games would be held there, it was agreed that Russian Railways would be responsible for constructing the railway network, which was hardly a surprise. Our company was already widely recognised for its ability to complete challenging infrastructure projects, having earned this reputation through the construction of the Ladozhsky railway station in St Petersburg, the Severomuysky Tunnel on the Baikal Amur Mainline (BAM), and the high-speed Sapsan train between Moscow and St Petersburg, to name just a few. What was somewhat more unusual was that, after a certain amount of consideration in the Ministry of Transport, they decided that Russian Railways should also be responsible for the parallel automotive road construction.

Russian Railways were involved in the development plans from the beginning, our brief steadily expanding to include roads and railway lines (notably the creation of the main passenger artery for the Sochi Olympics, a combined road–rail connection between Adler and Alpika, as well as redeveloping the 90-mile-long Tuapse–Adler rail line, which in places was already nearly a hundred years old and only single track); modernising existing train stations and, where necessary, building new ones from scratch. We were also tasked with creating a shuttle service between Sochi and Sochi airport, and developing high-speed electric trains. As each of these new tasks arrived we created a plan for them which was then submitted for approval to both the government and Russian Olympic Committee.

Everything had to be ready by 2012, so that test games and other events could be held in all the stadiums throughout 2013. It helped that I had a useful quantity of personal experience in this field, notably with the construction of the port complex at Ust-Luga. But, of course, every endeavour on this scale is different. For instance, the Ust-Luga development was conducted against a mixture of apathy and hostility – you could be forgiven for feeling sometimes that most people were unaware that the work was taking place, and of the small proportion of people who did know about it, an even smaller proportion cared whether it was a success – whereas from almost the first day of our involvement in Sochi, there was widespread interest at every level of Russian society. Nevertheless, we did not need to be told that enthusiasm by itself is not sufficient to build railways or stations; there was no doubt that the task ahead of us would be unprecedentedly challenging and complex.

Perhaps there is an 'ideal' mega-project out there, an endeavour characterised by a limitless budget, a generous deadline for completion, compliant local authorities and a landscape free of geographical bear traps, but I have yet to see one. Far more commonly, one sees substantial delays, or budgets that spiral out of control – Eurotunnel and the new Berlin airport are good examples of this. Generally, as a CEO in these situations, you find yourself acting as a kind of risk-assessment manager as much as a strategist. Your role, insofar as it is possible, is to anticipate the problems that the project you are responsible for is likely to run into, and to then take steps that will allow you to cut them at their roots (ideally), or (more realistically) cope with them if they grow. These issues might, very broadly, be divided into three categories: geography, humanity and uncertainty.

The natural environment you will be working in – its topography, weather, the actual composition of the landscape – has a potentially enormous impact on the way in which your project will unfold. I have always believed that building and maintaining infrastructure is an organic process that has to be responsive to nature's reactions. The world around us does not consist of inert matter; it is a living body with which we interact constantly. Look at the way it has reacted to the decades' worth of pollutants we have pumped into the atmosphere. It is easy to regard a section of steel railway track, to take an example pertinent to my career, as something immutable that will behave the same way wherever it is placed. But in fact as soon as it is laid, it will begin communicating with the ground below it: together, soil, metal and gravel form a complex mechanism. Any enterprise that does not take this into account is guaranteed to fail.

In this instance the most immediate challenge was presented by the vertiginous mountains that surrounded the resort. It was these as much as anything that had hindered the city's development over the past couple of decades. We also knew that part of the route for the combined road and railway had to follow the River Mzymta's valley, which would make for a picturesque journey, but also a winding and circuitous one, adding substantially to the length of road and track we needed to build. And because of the challenging topography, we knew that as much as two thirds of the highway would be made up of bridges, overpasses and tunnels – each presenting their own very particular logistical and technical challenges.

Another issue that we had to plan for in advance was the Tuapse–Adler rail line. Parts of it ran along the coast, which was threatened by two significant environmental factors that promised both to frustrate the construction itself and to present a level of risk that would hang like the Sword of Damocles over the railway's future operations if we did not take care to resolve them.

There was the danger of rocks cascading down from the cliffs above the shore, and from below there was the substantial risk of water damage by waves. It was plain that reinforcing and making the lines safe by international standards required hefty investment. We all knew that there was no way we could proceed while there was still the possibility of whole slabs of the mountain – stones, earth, trees – destroying everything in its path as they crashed down. I saw this happen three times myself, but just once was enough to convince me that it was imperative we took every step available to secure the slopes so that, even in times of heavy rainfall, the track would be safe from landslides. Huge quantities of concrete and Olympian-sized steel pylons now provide a kind of backbone to the crumbling mountainside.

The problem with the water was perhaps not as dramatic, but

no less important. We were given notice of the potential strength of the tide when the feeder port that they had built to supply the construction materials for the Sochi Olympics (worth over 800 million roubles) was washed down in a storm, something that ensured that the responsibility for transporting the construction materials for the project fell almost entirely onto our shoulders. Because the coast was so exposed to the potentially ruinous impact of the local tides, we ended up having to pour 800,000 tonnes of gravel every year onto the beaches to protect the tracks.

One thing that is rarely taken into account when people consider a big infrastructure project like Sochi is that there is only ever a certain amount of resources to go round, whether it be materials, machinery or human beings. This is especially true when you know that everyone involved is working to the same tight deadline as you are. In fact, one of the first signs that this was going to be an unusually difficult enterprise came during the planning stage. Or, to be more precise, the warning came because there was not going to be a planning stage; at least, not as we recognised it. The usual calculation is that the planning stage lasts two years, and that the costs incurred during this period comprise approximately 10 per cent of the price of the entire project. In theory, this enables the company not only to ensure that they've had time to produce a blueprint for the project that identifies and minimises all potential risks, but also that it gives them the opportunity to procure essential staff, equipment and raw materials. We did not have this privilege; we had to use materials the second they were ready. Normally, the production of materials, the planning and the construction of the project occur successively. In Sochi, they ran in parallel.

I remember that one day we were preparing for a visit from President Putin to the Olympic Park. All that remained to be finished was a small stretch of no more than 300m. It should have been an easy task, but then, all of a sudden, we learned that the delivery of asphalt we had been expecting had been taken by one of the other companies working on the project. There was huge panic everywhere – how could we convince the President that we were on top of our work if the first thing he saw was an unfinished road? We could not very well tell him that we had been unable to obtain the necessary materials. What kind of message would that have sent to him?

While we hadn't foreseen this particular problem, we knew that very few things ever go to plan. So Russian Railways contracted entire plants to provide certain materials, including asphalt. This meant that we could operate as efficiently as possible, but also that we had contingency measures in place to deal with these sorts of problems – the kind that are 'unimaginable' until they actually take place. In the nick of time, we managed to turn around some of our own cars, which were carrying asphalt to other places, and used this to finish the last few metres. The next morning, when the President and his entourage arrived, their cars could drive across these brand-new asphalt roads, every last man unaware of what had taken place the night before.

As important as it is to engage fully with the ecology and landscape in which you will be operating, or the resources you have to hand, no project will ever be a success without the contributions of other people: there will always be a 'human factor'. Ultimately, unless you are able to convince others – whether that is politicians, colleagues or members of the public – of the merits of your endeavour, then your chances of seeing it through to completion will be vastly reduced. In the case of Sochi, we knew that an infrastructure development on the scale we had planned would inevitably cause profound levels of disruption, so we had to continue to fulfil our many responsibilities to the people of the city, both those who lived in the region throughout the year, and also the large numbers who came to work for just the summer. We made sure that passenger operations – both long-distance and intercity services – continued to run, no matter how great the upheaval caused by the Olympic work. And while we knew that once everything began in earnest we would not be able to prevent roads from being blocked, or avoid creating unwelcome noise and pollution that would disrupt daily life and discourage tourists from coming to the resorts, we did what we could to mitigate the unhappiness this had the potential to cause. Representatives from Russian Railways met with different local citizens' groups to explain what we were doing, talking them through every aspect of our endeavours to show them that even the service roads were necessary. In doing so, we were, eventually, able to secure their support.

Another part of the 'human factor' is your ability to negotiate with administrative entities. Every country and region has an administrative ecology that is just as particular to it as its natural geography. I have lost count of the number of construction projects I have seen crushed at birth by oppressive Russian legislation and the proliferation of organs responsible for implementing it. More often than not, you are required, at least in theory, to secure preliminary permission to start work, but because this process takes a huge amount of time to complete, and involves exchanges with a plethora of different agencies, you can end up waiting for so long that it risks seriously damaging your enterprise's prospects. As a result, most constructors start work without the appropriate permits, and hope that they'll be able to pick them up along the way.

For instance, the area around Sochi in which we were supposed to be creating the infrastructure was a designated conservation region. You could not even cut a tree over there without getting permission first, and industrial activity was prohibited. So even before the first hole could be dug, we had to introduce special amendments to the Law On Specially Protected Natural Territories, and have them passed by the Duma. Then, once the state was content for us to begin, we knew we would have to deal with the local authorities. One example of how complex, even maddening, these interactions could be arrived when we needed to create a service road on the left bank of the river where there were a handful of houses, but not even a track to connect them to the outside world. According to the federal environmental protection laws, after finishing the work, we were supposed to rip the tarmac up and restore everything back to how it was, which is what, with a somewhat heavy heart, we agreed to do. However, during the final stages of the project, the residents, who almost overnight had been given the means to travel easily to Sochi and beyond, demanded that the road should be kept once we'd moved on. Which is, of course, a useful illustration of how capable human beings are of springing a surprise or two.

This brings us neatly to the third and most challenging category: the things that cannot be predicted. There are some events that you can neither anticipate nor prevent, and being able to step up when your company activity veers outside its normal modus operandi is one of the defining features of a good CEO. Life does not provide you with a complete script for every breath you take, and when you find yourself exposed to abnormal, unprecedented situations that are not covered by existing legislation and procedures, you cannot afford to lose your head or be afraid of taking risks.

However, you can at least introduce prophylactic measures. Sochi is within spitting distance of places like Abkhazia, Ossetia, Georgia and Chechnya, territories that, while peaceful at the time, all had a recent history of violence and discontent, and we had to safeguard our supposedly idyllic resort against the possibility of a terrorist attack. To this end, we installed a special system of around-the-clock observation and security, which included video surveillance, fences, dedicated security centres. Under Russian law, the owner of the infrastructure is responsible for its protection. The security services made recommendations and we were compelled to follow them, no matter how expensive they were.

Another potentially lethal threat came from the fact that Sochi is situated in an area that has historically been particularly vulnerable to earthquakes, something which had to be considered during our planning and construction. But if we could at least conceive that a terrorist attack or volcanic eruption *might* occur, there are always predicaments that, like Donald Rumsfeld's infamous 'unknown unknowns', leap out at you, seemingly out of nowhere, halfway through the project or just as you are about to cut the ribbon to celebrate its completion.

Over the next few years we would be hit by one unexpected

event after another. Some, like the financial crisis in 2008, impacted upon the rest of the country, while others affected only us (who could have predicted we would have to purchase five million fish to preserve a river's fragile ecology, or search for different ways to keep the Olympic Flame alight in windy conditions?).

It was not long before it became clear that our problems with drilling tunnels were not limited to trying to find the right equipment. My Vice President, Oleg Toni, the same person who had alerted me to the first issues with the Dragon's Mouth, came to me again and he told me:

> You need to know this. We have discovered that the geological picture which we were given was incomplete, and in the course of our work on Tunnel Complex No. 3 we've learned that once you get a certain distance inside the mountain's skin you begin to hit a substance like powder.

We were, he said, operating in Karst topography, a landscape shaped by the effects of underground water on soluble stone, which meant that it was honeycombed by caves and sinkholes. This meant that each section of the tunnel we were drilling was effectively unique and had to be tackled individually: the engineers would not know exactly what they were dealing with until they had made their first incursions into it.

It was almost a paradox; you would have thought that the softer the rock, the easier it would be to tunnel through. But what was actually happening was that the drills were set up to rotate at a velocity sufficient to excavate incredibly hard materials, but when working with this powdery rock, the drills did not encounter the same resistance, so they simply spun faster, faster, faster, faster, until they reached temperatures of up to 1,400 degrees, which also happens to be the point that metal begins to melt. Although there were sophisticated electronic monitoring systems that were supposed to regulate the operating temperature of each drill, the changes came so quickly that the machines could not respond in time. It ended up with the metal solidifying with this powder-like substance and thus preventing the blades from rotating. It was very hard to free the equipment afterwards. No matter how methodical we tried to be, no matter how many sophisticated new technologies we tried to use, we were caught on the horns of an age-old dilemma: if you do not know what to look for, how are you supposed to find it?

In the end we had to use an awkward, time-consuming combination of drilling and blowing if we wanted to make any kind of progress without permanently damaging the equipment. We would drill horizontal holes to try and anticipate what lay ahead.

Progress was slow, and then one day my deputy came to me again, very tense, and said:

> Listen, we only have 150m of the tunnel left to excavate, and at this moment, I cannot be 100 per cent sure that, although we are exerting as much control over every moment as we can, we will not encounter unstable cavities again. And if that happens, then I can guarantee you that a major part of the equipment will fail.

He carried on and explained that there was only one company in the world – a Canadian company – that would be able to repair the machinery in the event of this taking place.

We can hire them so that if our machinery falls victim to this threat then they will be on the spot immediately, in time to fix it before the delay will wreak havoc on our capacity to meet our deadlines. If we hire them and the machinery doesn't fail, then we're just wasting a huge pile of cash.

As before, I knew that it was not fair that a decision like that should rest on his shoulders. If your decision left Russian Railways unable to complete, then you would be responsible for blowing up the entire Olympic Games infrastructure and arrangements. If it comes to nothing, then you are the boy who cried wolf. You have landed a company that is already investing huge amounts of money into the project with a redundant bill. That was a dreadful time. I was trailed constantly by heavy feelings of anxiety and some days I did not feel anything beyond a persistent obligation to the task I had been given, but it would only be later, when I looked in the mirror, or into the faces of those friends who had studied my face with concern, that I realised how tense and exhausted I truly was.

As it turned out we eventually alighted upon an unexpected solution for our problem with the mountain at Deep Yar Waterfall, but I do not think anyone could ever claim it was easy. For over twenty-five years, Russian Railways had used huge tunnel-boring machines (also known as TBMs, or moles, for obvious reasons) to excavate the Severomuysky Tunnel in Siberia – at 15.3km, Russia's longest tunnel. They were behemoths, standing 10m high, 9m wide, 100m long, and weighing thousands of tonnes in total. It would have taken eight months, at least, for a piece of new equipment, one which could be adapted to excavate any kind of rock, to be delivered. Eight months we simply did not have. The only other option that I was presented with was flying one of the existing machines from Siberia via Altay to Italy, where its major components could be refurbished to perform the task at hand, and then back to Sochi. That is pretty much the equivalent of picking up a house, loading it onto a plane, and then carrying it thousands of miles. There was only one plane on the planet large enough to carry it: the Antonov 124-100, which normally moves trains. (I wonder how many people noticed the irony of this project being saved by a plane designed during the Soviet Union and built in Ukraine, with whom tensions were already ratcheting up.)

The enormous Antonov was a Soviet-style solution, one that, like the enterprise as a whole, relied on state intervention to succeed. I have yet to learn of an infrastructure company in the world that can make its living from commercial operations alone. Infrastructure by its very nature needs a substantial amount of government investment. For example, we calculated during the period of modernisation of BAM and Transsib that we needed 560 billion roubles, of which we could provide 360 billion roubles through our commercial activity. The rest had to be made up by the state. The situation was no different here. In the past we had been able to secure investment from private enterprise, but since companies with sufficient capital in Russia at the time were increasingly few and far between, we were ultimately reliant on cross-financing from the government.

All of the major Russian corporations (both those owned by the state and private enterprise) were involved in the process, but more than anything it was the unwavering political will to ensure that the Olympic Games was successful that provided everybody with the necessary momentum. In some ways, it was reminiscent of Ust-Luga, another PPP project in which the state made a very strong commitment.

Central to this was Dmitry Kozak, the deputy Prime Minister, who was faced by a monstrous task. On the one hand, he was overseeing the creation of an Olympic site in an area whose existing facilities and infrastructure were so minimal that the project was effectively one of building from the ground up. On the other hand, he needed to demonstrate to private businessmen that they could expect a return on the very substantial investment they were being asked to contribute – that the sporting and hospitality facilities, as well as the transport network, that were being constructed would all have a future beyond the winter of 2014. In parallel to this work, he was also responsible for the coordination of both state and local agencies, government ministries, corporations, banks, and, in conjunction with the specially created company 'Olympstroy', the Russian Olympic Committee.

Kozak was able to draw upon his legal background, vast experience in the civil service and government, and the support of the government, Duma and President to overcome the many obstacles facing him. He skilfully negotiated a path that cut through the objections over conservation, the layers of bureaucracy and local egoism, and introduced the special legislation, along with amendments to existing federal and local laws, that made the project possible. What we built was perhaps not perfect (what infrastructure development ever is?), and we made, and corrected, mistakes along the way, but if one considers the circumstances, as well as the end result, I still regard Sochi as a success.

In terms of scale, complexity, and pace of construction, there is nowhere anywhere in the world that is comparable to the work we completed in Sochi. The transport infrastructure was built in difficult engineering and geotechnical conditions with minimal disruption to the Sochi nature reserve's landscape, all of which necessitated ingenious, highly technical solutions (it was not for nothing that our work beneath the Dragon's Mouth was recognised with a prize at the 2011 International Tunnelling Awards).

And it was all completed under unbelievable pressure, both in terms of scrutiny and the immovable deadline we had to meet. In just five years, we built, among other things, 131km of railway and road; forty-six rail bridges and twenty-three road bridges; twelve tunnels; four new stations (and remodelled a further three); 37km of temporary roads; 43km of overhead power lines; a 2.8km shuttle connection between Adler and Sochi airport; a five-storey transport hub linking rail, road and water transport; railway freight yards; and a 49-room sanatorium complete with a five-star health resort. It is an achievement about which I feel incredibly proud. I remember that, after the Opening Ceremony, 40,000 people, who were supposed to be dispersed between buses and cars, rushed directly to the railway station. As I watched them surge towards the entrance I felt my heart trembling, but we managed it. Everything worked perfectly.

The infrastructure we created has contributed to the renaissance of Sochi's fortunes over the past ten years. Its transport network has been transformed completely, the city no longer looks like the ghost of its Soviet incarnation, and its environment is no longer afflicted by the pollution that once rendered its waters so unsavoury. Tourist numbers have almost returned to their pre-1991 levels, and it possible once more to consider it as our nation's 'summer capital'.

Sochi was not just a success for Russian Railways, but a symbol of Russia's own development. It would have been completely impossible to achieve what we did in Sochi in the volatile, fragmented climate of the 1990s. The legal system then was still in a state of flux; power was weak, dispersed. Different interest groups circled the President hungrily, each trying to push the country in a different direction, and the composition of the government changed as often as ladies' gloves. Chechnya, less than 300 miles from Sochi, had been consumed by a vicious civil war, one that to many seemed to presage the absolute disintegration of the rest of the country.

By the time that Sochi had won the right to host the Games, things were already completely different. President Putin and his government had managed to consolidate the state's authority and create a government that could actually govern, as well as prising power out of the hands of the oligarchs. By returning peace to Chechnya, they had also managed to prevent the further disintegration of the country. The economy was growing, and you could feel a new optimism in the general mood of society: young people were starting new businesses; there was a huge fall in capital-crime rates.

Much has already been said about the political nature of this iteration of the Winter Games, specifically in terms of Russia and the President's political authority.

The majority of the Russian population were opposed to the idea of using sport as an explicitly political vehicle – they wanted a 'clean' Olympics – but at the same time, people realised that it did offer an opportunity to, on the one hand, introduce the world to traditional Russian hospitality and dignity, and on the other, to use this grand project to consolidate the Russian economy and state institutions, and to consolidate Russian society as a whole. To my mind, these targets were achieved.

The Sochi Olympics should have been heralded as an achievement in itself, as well as a symbol of Russia's new vibrancy and confidence. The fact that we were able to put on such an impressive spectacle at all, given the many challenges faced, should have been cause for celebration, as was the fact that a record number of nations competed and that the host nation had topped the medal table.

But you would not know any of this from reading the foreign press coverage of the project. Perhaps this is unsurprising at a time when relations between Russia and much of the West were considered to be at their lowest since 1991, and would become still worse after Ukraine descended into civil war in the weeks immediately following the Games. A project that was supposed to have helped renew Russia's reputation was instead a lightning rod that attracted all kinds of assaults on our government's foreign and domestic policies.

Much of the criticism was directed at the construction of the infrastructure. We received scrutiny from Russian politicians and businessmen, and from every corner of Russian society. There were, of course, many objective people who provided necessary criticisms of a number of aspects of the organisation, planning and implementation of the Sochi Olympic Games project, but they were joined by other less circumspect people whose only aim was to secure popularity for themselves by passing on scurrilous rumours.

It is only now that I know for sure that there were powerful interests working to undermine the image not only of the project, but of the President himself, the man who was the driving force behind the whole Sochi enterprise. A vicious campaign, orchestrated by a Western PR company that was paid with money from Russia, was waged in the mass media against us, and it led to all kinds of aspersions being thrown on the actions of myself and Russian Railways. I have always believed that the press should at least try to provide a fair and complete picture of what went on, but with Sochi, I never had the feeling that the foreign mass media wanted, really and objectively, to understand the actual situation with the construction, or to provide useful criticism that might have been a spur to improvement. There was never any acknowledgement of the size of the task, the tightness of the deadline, or the unbelievable efforts the staff of Russian Railways made to complete their work. They never talked about the horrendous difficulties posed by the tunnel drilling, or the high standard of the accommodation we provided for those building the infrastructure.

I certainly never heard of any journalist coming to one of our building sites and asking the workers, 'Are you proud of what you are doing? Are you happy with the conditions in which you are living here?' All we heard was that Russian Railways had polluted the environment, that they had incurred costs that were absolutely abnormal, that their every transaction was infected by the most invidious strains of corruption. Those reporters knew the story they wanted to write before they ever asked their first question, and they never questioned whether there was any real substance behind it. But then it is so easy to talk when you have no responsibility for anything yourself; you can publish what you like and never give a second thought to the consequences.

You would also be surprised how rarely, if ever, they used professional sources. Even when they were able to talk to somebody who had a direct connection to Sochi operations, they were invariably a person who could shed light on only a small element of the entire project. No information they provided was ever put into proper context. So someone can check the internet, compare the costs of the construction of the Adler–Krasnaya Polyana railway line with the 'Canada Line' built in Vancouver, and see that we spent more. And from that small nugget they can draw all kinds of outlandish inferences about corruption and incompetence. However, if they had taken into account, for instance, the fact that our rail and road infrastructure was approximately six times the length of its Canadian equivalent, and that it was built despite huge geological and topographical handicaps, then their calculations would immediately begin to look completely different.

This cavalier approach to legitimate information was combined with deliberate attempts to introduce disinformation into discussions about the project. (Boris Nemtsov's claim that $30 billion was stolen was the most egregious example. We had decided to challenge his allegations in the courts, and were confident of winning, but his tragic murder stopped us in our tracks. We thought it would be appropriate to abide by an old Russian saying: 'If you have nothing good to say about the dead, then say nothing at all.' In retrospect, this was perhaps a mistake.)

There seems also to have been a widespread assumption that there was something opaque about the way we functioned; that we presented the state with our plans, took their cash and then worked in secrecy until we eventually presented them with the final results. In fact, the opposite was true.

For a start, we were working alongside Dmitry Kozak and Olympstroy's supervisory committee, and during the five-year period Russian Railways were engaged on this project, we were subject to over 1,500 inspections. There were visitors from the prosecutor's office, the tax office, the audit chamber of the parliament, law enforcement organisations – representatives from almost any branch of the federal and municipal governments you might care to mention. They came every day, they checked every part of every job, whether that was the price we were paying for a particular material or how we were approaching a particular engineering issue. It was a constant process of proving that our planning and our work were effective and in accordance with the particular demands of the Olympic Games, and also in accordance with Russia's construction laws.

The inspections were often the result of malicious gossip, but inevitably they had real consequences. For instance, one day I saw a very strongly worded letter from an FSB representative to the President, which informed him that, rather than installing special filters, we were pumping the waste water from our activities directly into the river. As soon as I read this letter, I called the Head of the Security Services and we arranged a group to go there to take samples of the water. We found out that it was completely false information.

It is also true, however, that although Sochi was, overall, a success, this does not mean that everything we did was perfect. How could it have been under the circumstances? We had so much ground to cover, so many challenges to overcome. But as much as the memory may still sting, I believe that it is important to spend time contemplating what went wrong, and why. There is little to be gained from pretending that one is infallible, and much more to be lost if one does not learn from the times when projects go awry.

There were logistical missteps that wasted valuable time and resources, such as the water pipe we built to supply a remote village that was destroyed as soon as heavy trucks began to drive over it. Other scenarios were more complex – reminders both that any intervention in a community's economy can have a welter of unforeseen consequences, and that the Russian government is not omnipotent, no matter what some people might believe. For instance, before the Olympics came to Sochi, the taxi services there were run by a kind of local administrative mafia who exerted a menacing level of control. During the construction process, when 25,000 law officers descended upon the region, the mafia became invisible. So much so that we allowed ourselves to believe that they had disappeared for ever.

But once we had moved on, we began to hear stories about train drivers being intimidated by men who told them that if they performed their services as usual, then they would return home to find their houses burnt down. The infrastructure we built brought many benefits to the local community, but the fact that train journeys were twenty times cheaper than travelling by taxi meant that the cab drivers' livelihoods, as well as those of the mafia who purported to represent their interests, had been hit hard. The local administration have been able to do little to reassure potential train drivers that they will be protected if they carry out their duties, so we have been left with an almost brand-new rail network on which very few people feel safe enough to work. Without any drivers, there can be no trains.

In retrospect it was perhaps obvious that this would have occurred. However, you can sometimes become so focused attending to a particular problem (in this case the overwhelming urgency of having everything ready for the Olympics) that you forget that the solution might have its own unwanted consequences.

It is in situations like that that you find yourself wishing you could have your time again. Suddenly, it becomes obvious what you *should* have done. The fog clears and solutions present themselves with perfect clarity, but of course it is too late. You have to accept that you have made a mistake. Your chance to prevent it from occurring again has long since slipped through your fingers, and yet you have at least been left with something: experience. This humbling reminder of one's own limitations is the hardest-won kind of knowledge.

Most lives are full of hugely varied experiences, each of which plays its own role in forming one's character. I have worked as both an entrepreneur and servant of the state, steadily learning a huge amount about everything from transport and education to governance. In St Petersburg during the '90s, I was part of an innovative, forward-thinking business community; at the North-West Inspectorate, I received a practical education in how state and municipal institutions functioned; my experiences at Ust-Luga taught me how to plan and manage a complex infrastructure project; and my time at the Ministry of Transport sometimes felt like I had returned to university. I gleaned a great deal too from those years involved with Sochi. But if there is any consistent principle that is true for every stage of my career, then it is this: there is an almost unbridgeable gulf between theory and practice. You can think that you are just getting to grips with the task in front of you, that you understand it from every angle and are in control, and then circumstances intervene, and in the blink of an eye you find yourself having to come to terms with a role that has mutated out of all recognition.

In Russia, a country whose economy and society is in a constant state of transition, the picture is always partial; one is never presented with a complete plan of the terrain before you, the kind that might show you which route to take, and allow you to avoid missteps. It is only with hindsight that what was right and what was wrong become clear. I have come to understand that there are limits to what we can ever truly know, and limits too on what we can control.

When I was in St Petersburg working as a civil servant during the late '90s, I learned that 5 per cent of your activity will always go awry. You cannot account for every piece of gravel, or every kilo of cement. The same is true for a big system like the railways; indeed, the more complex the system, the greater the chance of deviation. One must accommodate oneself to the knowledge that at any moment, somewhere within the system, there will be accidents; that somebody will be making the wrong decision, that there will be shortages of manpower or equipment. Before I began at Russian Railways, there was not even a procedure for recording derailings: they were so frequent, and happened in places so remote from our centre of operations, that there was no point.

Ultimately, these small incidents of chaos were not sufficient to affect the workings of the system as a whole, so they could be absorbed. To try to change this and achieve a pristine model of management is, I have come to understand, a futile quest – one that would consume untold amounts of your energy and resources for little or no reward.

Of course this does not mean that responsibility can be abdicated entirely. It would be criminal to neglect security, the comfort and wellbeing of your customers and staff and the safety of the cargo and the operations. But elsewhere, you have to make this accommodation with reality, with the many loose ends within the railway system that simply cannot or will not be tied. You have to accept that somewhere in one of the more remote corners of the country, one of your functionaries is likely to be abusing his power, and that unless he makes a mistake or gets too greedy, there will be little you can do to stop him. It was no different in the days of the Soviet Union, where people would come to special arrangements with their boss, or the men and women who ran local food stores, in an attempt to gain small advantages that would make their life that little bit easier. It was not consistent with the regime's ideology, nor was it legal, but nevertheless it was a persistent feature of life under communism. Russia resists any attempt to micromanage it; you cannot regulate every breath.

In Sochi, almost the sole circumstance that did not change was the one we might most fervently have wished could be amended: the date by which our work absolutely had to be finished. Years later, when all the dust had settled, I talked with my friends, the CEOs of the foreign railways in France or Germany, about what we were faced with, the sheer range of challenges. They told me, shaking their heads, that it would be completely impossible to create that infrastructure on that timetable in the West. In Russia, the only thing that was impossible was that we should fail to meet our deadline.

But there was another thing that we had not anticipated. Sochi would be, though we did not know it at a time, the last example of this kind of grand-scale infrastructure we undertook. Storm clouds were gathering, and events outside my control were already beginning to conspire against us.

CHAPTER SEVEN

IRREVOCABLE MISTAKES

Much ink has been spilled about my departure from Russian Railways in 2015: fanciful, lurid allegations have been made against me and members of my family; speculations that belong to the world of political dramas. The circumstances surrounding my exit are not replete with the kinds of details that might interest tabloid papers, but there is much in the narrative that I believe will be of interest to anyone curious about the ways in which Russia and its politics work. And I do not know if this counts as a plot twist, but little of what happened was a surprise to me – I saw it coming.

It was in September 2013, after eight years as president of Russian Railways, that I realised my time there was nearing its end. The Russian economy was under pressure; growth had slowed to just over 1 per cent and the value of the rouble was falling. Perhaps even more so than after the global financial crisis of 2008, it felt as if we had begun to exist within a completely unprecedented set of circumstances. Twelve months earlier, in his famous May Decrees, President Putin had promised the

Russian people that spending on social welfare would remain high. The pressures on the government were mounting by the day, and everyone looking on knew that, before long, something would have to give.

The new conditions had already announced themselves within the offices of Russian Railways. It was not just that the atmosphere was changing – though you could sense it shifting, almost by the second – but that our ambitions were being circumscribed, our ability to act decisively pinched. Nobody could agree on the measures that needed to be taken to get the Russian economy back on track. The Ministry of Finance was vociferously arguing for a cut in tariffs – the prices the railways charge to private businesses to transport their goods across the country – in the belief that it would cut inflation. I was doing everything I could to make the case for increased investment in the economy, a programme that would give private business the opportunity to make money by building infrastructure. We waited anxiously for the budget due that September, when a decision about what path to take was to be made, hoping that it would bring relief.

The months leading up to the announcement were filled with the usual lobbying, harassing and horse-trading by the country's various ministries and its state-owned companies, each anxious to secure the share they felt their contribution to the nation deserved – a process made all the more feverish by the fact that the straitened economic situation had substantially diminished the pot. But in 2013, there was more at stake than ever in the budget allocations. Some of the most prolonged, energetic debates went further, interrogating the most fundamental questions facing our country. In the midst of a recession, what fiscal model would serve Russia best? Do you spend your way out of trouble, or is retrenchment the best answer? How active a role should the state play in the nation's economic life?

The fiercest arguments played out, as they always do in Russia, behind closed doors. On one occasion, I was making so much noise at a meeting at the Ministry of Finance that the President invited some of us to sit down together to try to settle the matter. It was a closed circle, limited to the Minister for Economic Development, the Minister of Finance, the deputy Prime Minister, a representative from the presidential administration and, of course, Mr Putin. Even here, though, I struggled to control myself. The finance minister and I held completely opposing views, with neither of us willing to cede an inch to the other. At one moment, in an attempt to put my point across, I betrayed the frustration that had been building up inside me for what seemed like years: 'You are the Minister of Finance,' I told Anton Siluanov,[16] 'so you should at least be familiar with all four of the rules of arithmetic, not just division and subtraction.' I received a calm but firm reprimand from the President for my outburst, and yet what stung most was the knowledge that, for the first time since taking over at Russian Railways, it felt as if I had been left on the losing side of the argument. It seemed that the shift in the political weather meant that I was no longer the right man for the job.

Sometimes it can seem as if the discussions Russians have about the railways are also conversations about the kind of nation they

---

16 Mr Siluanov replaced Mr Kudrin in 2011, after the latter was asked to resign by the then President Dmitry Medvedev.

want to be. There is a famous legend about the city of Tobolsk, once one of Siberia's most important cities. When the Trans-Siberian railway was first being discussed, the local merchants bribed officials in St Petersburg to prevent the new route from passing through their city. They were concerned that the trains would strain the nerves of the horses that were a key element in the local economy. Their money talked, and within a matter of years, Tobolsk slipped into the byways of history to become a quaint, well-preserved backwater, while Novosibirsk, its economy supercharged by the railways, became Siberia's capital and is now Russia's third-most populous city.

If felt as if something similar happened as we embarked on our own efforts to ensure that the Russian railway system, and by extension the nation's economy, was equipped to deal with the accelerated demands of the twenty-first century. By talking about how the railways might be reformed and run, people from across the political spectrum were able to also talk more generally about the way in which the country should be governed.

Most models are wrong, a handful are useful, but there are others that are lethal. Russia has felt the awful truth of this more than once in the past century. For two decades now, Russia's history – at least domestically – has been dominated by arguments about what kind of model, or what combination of models, should be used to determine the country's future.

In the years that followed the dissolution of the Soviet Union, the momentum within the Kremlin was decisively behind those who wanted to treat Russia as a tabula rasa, one they could inscribe with the economic wisdom that, they believed, had ensured the success of the free-marketeering Western powers. Boris Yeltsin, surrounded by neo-liberals such as Anatoly Chubais, and oligarchs like Boris Berezovsky, was broadly speaking in favour of the sweeping changes that his inner circle urged upon him, even though the chaos over which he presided was perhaps not the best environment to attempt what was, in effect, an economic experiment.

Outside of Yeltsin's inner circle, however, people were considerably more circumspect about the potential of this model to transform their lives, and the electoral success of the Communist Party's successors throughout the '90s was a testament to the enduring appeal of the policies it was seen to stand for. This scepticism was given an even sharper edge once the population at large became fully acquainted with the disastrous privatisations that had, for many, come to symbolise the greed, incompetence and corruption of the men who led their country.

Things were different in the new millennium – or at least that is what we told ourselves. There was little debate as to the necessity of modernising the economy; everyone knew how important it was, but before long there was profound disagreement about the route we should be taking to achieve it. It was a practical as much as an ideological conflict.

A younger generation of reformers, unbruised by the catastrophes of the previous decade, still believed that they could transform everything, invent a new Russia free from the neuroses and stagnation that, as they saw it, had been hindering its progress. The problem was not, they said, that there had been too much privatisation. Quite the opposite; there had not been enough.

They found a congenial home in Vladimir Putin's administration, which in large part committed itself to continuing the liberalising reforms that its predecessor had tried to implement. The government was honeycombed by zealous neoliberals – many of whom had been appointed by Yeltsin's administration – whose overriding aim was to transform Russia into a Western-style economy run along the purest of free-market principles. In the process, they would shrink the state, introduce competition into sectors that had previously been governed as monopolies, render every element of our governance transparent, and clear away all the obstructive debris left by the old order.

The 'young' reformers of the early 2000s had read Western textbooks, and some of them had even studied in Western universities, but even though they were now in their forties, they did not know what it was like to run a factory, or to manage the complicated interactions between infrastructure and industry.

Their superficial knowledge was accompanied by a pronounced superciliousness about the professional experience of those who had helped to administer the Soviet Union. While the march of events had diminished the relevance of much of their theoretical knowledge, their practical knowledge – including but certainly not limited to their recall of the mistakes they had made and the lessons they had learned from them – had profound value. But the accumulated wisdom of the old state's administrators was often discarded by the reformers; it seemed that, for them at least, the lessons of history were too knotty, too resistant to the pristine economic models they had learned about to be of much use.

During Putin's first years in government, the discussions about the modernisation of Russia began, increasingly, to focus on

Russian Railways. There had long been an agreement that, along with a great proportion of our country's economic apparatus, the railway system needed to be reformed, but no real consensus as to how this might be implemented. As with every other sector of the economy, the railway system had suffered profoundly in the years after the fall of the Soviet Union.

The steep decline in industrial production led to a corresponding fall in rail traffic. At the same time, investment had been reduced substantially and the rolling stock had become old-fashioned, dangerous and unable to carry the amount of freight that was needed to sustain the Russian economy. The Railway Ministry also struggled to cope with the competition posed by new private operators who, as part of the general economic reforms that the country was being subjected to, were able to enter the market.

One example from 1995 illustrates how parlous the situation of this persistently profligate enterprise had become. That year, the Railway Ministry's cash flow dried up almost completely, and civil servants from Moscow had to stuff suitcases full of cash and travel to the provinces in order to pay employees' wages. At times, they were even reduced to bartering services for salaries.

However, what impressed me when I was appointed ten years later was how successful they had been at preserving the morale and professionalism that had always been a distinguishing feature of the railwaymen. Without any significant financial or political support, they had somehow ensured that the service still continued, just about, to function. After the dissolution of the Soviet Union, the infrastructure of many of the country's great monopolies fell apart, but the Railway Ministry had managed to keep intact even the network of professional universities and schools across the country that trained their engineers and workers.

Perhaps this should not have come as a huge surprise. Throughout our history, the railway workers have been an embodiment of the best aspects of Russia, considered to be the civil service's nonpareil – under the tsars, they unofficially enjoyed the same celebrated elite status as the navy did within the armed services; both institutions were a locus for national pride.

They might have been paid a little more than their counterparts in other wings of the state, they might have had a smart uniform and the right to travel for free, but the pride felt by a railway engineer, a station master or a locomotive driver was derived from their devotion to their work and their knowledge of its importance. The employees cherished the fact that they had all received a special education, that the job was day and night without any excuses, that they were subject to an almost military discipline. It would never be possible to overestimate the devotion displayed by the men and women who have been employed by the railways.

These were the people who worked, without a second thought for their own safety, on the front line in the conflicts that have defined the last century and a half of our history. During the war with Japan in 1905, an American journalist wrote that the Minister of Railways was more dangerous to the Japanese than his counterpart in the Ministry of Defence. The contribution the railwaymen made to that ultimately doomed, quixotic campaign was almost the only thing from it we can look back on with any pride. Tracks were laid across frozen rivers and lakes. Throughout the harsh winter, trains carried munitions and materiel, even submarines, to the hard-pressed soldiers fighting on what must have seemed like the other side of the world.

Just over forty years later, the great Marshal Georgy Zhukov would echo these sentiments when he suggested that Russia's defeat of the Third Reich was due in no small part to the effort and courage displayed by the railway workers. I was struck when I became CEO of Russian Railways by how resilient this spirit was – how completely it had survived the collapse of the Soviet Union as well as the years of neglect and decay that followed.

The minister responsible, Nikolai Aksenenko, was forced to retire in 2002 amid a storm of accusations about financial irregularities, but he had been a leader able to keep his organisation from disintegrating at a time of incredible pressure. He fought for the railways, and helped keep them together, making sure that even at times of accelerated regional tension, the CIS railway union, one of the USSR's most valuable legacies, remained solid. I would also come to understand that he was a far-sighted figure: many of the reforms we eventually implemented had been discussed by him years before.

Mr Aksenenko knew that times and technology had moved on and the old ministry was no longer constituted in such a way that would enable it to engage in building the large infrastructure projects – such as high-speed rail lines and new routes connecting natural resources to global markets – that we all understood would be a crucial part of the country's recovery. He tried to initiate a debate about introducing a more pronounced commercial element into the ministry's activities as early as 1992, and would continue to raise the principle throughout his tenure.

But he was acting in circumstances that were not friendly to such an ambitious undertaking. For one thing, the effort expended in ensuring that the railways continued to function and remained solvent left little energy for strategic thinking. And although his proposals were discussed in the Duma and by the country's nascent business elite, they never went very far. The political influence of his patron, Yeltsin (Aksenenko was part of the former president's close personal circle), was vanishing, and as a result, power in the country was fragmented. There may have been a set of compelling reasons to embark on far-reaching structural changes to the railways and the way they operated, but neither Aksenenko nor anyone else in the government had the political capital, or perhaps the energy, to push it through in the face of strong resistance from the resurgent Communist Party. Especially since everybody understood how complex and demanding a process it would be to modernise what had been known in the Soviet Union as the 'Empire inside the Empire'. This was not just because the vast, sprawling railway system employed so many people and possessed so many assets, it was also because the rail infrastructure was intimately linked with so many other industries. It is no coincidence that in the main it was the comparatively discrete, small-scale sectors of the economy that were first privatised. Nor is it a surprise that oligarchs on the hunt for easy profits left this challenging sector of the economy alone.

Only after Aksenenko had been ousted in 2002, when the country was in a much more satisfactory economic and political position, and the resistance to modernisation had largely subsided, was the possibility of reforming the railways discussed again.

President Putin supported the argument that the railways were central to Russia's revival; that Russia's natural resources – buried in remote, land-locked parts of the country – could be better exploited if they could be transported to the ports and on to markets more efficiently. The wellbeing of the railway system and the Russian economy were, as they always have been, intimately linked: if the railway system was not given the tools it needed to take on the modern world's challenges, then the country would suffer.

I had never expected to be charged with controlling Russia's railway system. In 2002 I was still deputy Minister of Transport, where I was responsible for trying to put back together the fragmented pieces of Russia's transport infrastructure, trying to find a way of integrating the railway system with the country's ports. I was already familiar with its staff and also the most essential aspects of their strategic planning and operations. More pertinently, I was in regular contact with the so-called 'Leningrad diaspora', or the *Piterskie* ('the Petersburgers'), as they are sometimes also known. They included, among others, Vladimir Putin, Herman Gref, Alexei Kudrin and Dmitry Kozak – men who had relocated to Moscow after the defeat of Anatoly Sobchak, and had moved into some of the country's top political positions.

On a Sunday afternoon in 2002, I received a call from the President, who asked my opinion about a particular individual who worked at the Ministry of Railways. Because this conversation was taking place so soon after the departure of Aksenenko, I immediately realised that the person the President was asking questions about was being considered as a replacement for the outgoing minister.

I knew the man in question from my previous work in St Petersburg and was not convinced he would be the right choice, so my responses were generally cagey, even negative. The President's next question took me by surprise: 'So, who *do* you think is suitable for the role?'

I told him that the only person whom I knew to be of the necessary calibre, even though I was not acquainted with him personally, was Gennady Fadeev, who was at the time head of Moscow Railways.

'Contact him, please. Make sure he is willing to accept the job.'

It was not long before I received another call from Mr Putin, this time to tell me that I was to become first deputy Minister of the Railways, reporting to Mr Fadeev, the minister. I did not know it then, but perhaps the most important phase of my professional life was about to begin.

Towards the end of President Putin's first term in office, it was decided that control over the management of the rail networks should pass from the Railways Ministry to a state-owned company with responsibility to make a profit. And so, in September 2003, Joint-Stock Company Russian Railways was created, and six months later, by presidential decree, the Ministry of Railways was abolished.

This was in itself already a far-reaching reform, but when I was appointed as the company's president in 2005, the pace at which we were working was accelerated. Broadly speaking, the strategy was to introduce the reforms that were needed to develop competition within the industry, facilitate private investment in rolling stock to renew the fleet, and help the railway system play a part in the infrastructure projects that were a central part of the country's economic strategy. All discussions and considerations of the best way to reform were permitted, but I was given one clear directive by Mr Putin when I was appointed: we were not to commit irrevocable mistakes.

In Russia, the railways and the economy are part of the same living organism. The railways' ability to work efficiently is inextricably bound up with every sector of the economy, and indeed with the lives of every single one of Russia's citizens. It carries a significant proportion of the nation's freight, employs a million of its citizens (more than any other commercial entity), and the country's people, especially on its remote peripheries, rely on trains to an extraordinary degree. We were to be guided by the same principles as a surgeon performing an operation. If we severed the wrong nerve ending, or removed the wrong organ, then the impact on this incredibly intricate, interlinked complex – comprising not just the rolling stock, track and stations, but power supply, communication networks, traffic and safety management systems – could be catastrophic.

The most significant element that needed the Kremlin's approval was, unsurprisingly, the shape that the reforms of Russian Railways would take. We were not responsible for making the final decision – what we were charged with was providing a suite of different proposals, each backed up with an arsenal of evidence, analysis and expert opinion so that they could not be simply dismissed out of hand.

There were a number of recent examples for us to follow, or avoid, both from close to home and from further afield. Towards the end of Putin's first term, a few sectors of the economy had already been transformed, with varying degrees of success. The government had long wanted to reorganise the sprawling monopolies that were such a dominant, and perhaps stifling, element of the country's economic landscape, and this process began in earnest soon after the turn of the century.

However, while the reformation of the oil industry had been largely successful, the modernisation of the energy and power-generation sectors was disastrous. For instance, the incompetent handling of the privatisation of the energy sector meant that the industry has been unable to make the substantial investments needed to improve, or even maintain, its infrastructure. For a long time, blackouts big enough to stop half the trains in Siberia from running were common. It was clear that a programme of modernisation did not always translate into increased efficiency. The experience was also a vivid reminder of how complex and fraught the process of transforming a national monopoly was likely to prove.

We were also alive to the experience of other nations who had attempted a similar process with their own railway systems. In Great Britain, for example, John Major's government attempted to implement a very pure model of privatisation. The result was a disjointed rail network, which lacked coordination and did not deliver the expected benefits in terms of efficiency and costs, and led ultimately to two devastating crashes and the loss of a great number of lives.

So we had seen how this approach could lead to a serious setback in the development and operations of the railways, and thus we knew that if we wanted to protect our passengers and ensure that our railway system would be able to stay abreast of the fierce demands of a 21st-century economy then we had to explore other options. It was also abundantly clear to us that no model of modernisation fits all railways. They are not like off-the-peg suits that can fit any customer; the reforms must reflect local conditions.

To this end, we employed all of the leading management consultants – including Ernst & Young, McKinsey & Co. and BCG – to present us with a range of alternative approaches. Their voices were joined by government ministers, members of the Duma and civil servants, all of whom had their own priorities. We also consulted with customers (the people who would actually be using the service), businessmen and the companies that built the locomotives and carriages on which our system depended.

To a large extent, I relied on my own intuition when evaluating the recommendations that were put before us. But I was anxious at every stage to draw as heavily as I could on the expertise of the industry's veterans, especially as there were influential groups from across the political spectrum who were keen to influence the nature and scope of the reforms.

Those pushing for an extreme model of reform that would culminate in a launch on the stock market included familiar faces such as Herman Gref at the Ministry of Economic Development and Trade, and Alexei Kudrin at the Ministry of Finance, as well as the experts in their orbits, most notably the civil servants who worked in the Anti-Monopoly Committee. Ranged against them were those who wished to preserve as much as possible of the state apparatus that we'd inherited from the Soviet Union, such as the former Prime Minister Nikolai Ryzhkov. I had to act as a bridge between all of these competing factions, to moderate both the potentially destructive instincts of the reformers and the ossified mentality of those who were determined to cling on to the old ways of running the country.

If I had any particular advantage going into the complex process of deciding the future of the railways, it was that having spent time working as both an entrepreneur and a servant of the state, and having seen how fruitfully the PPP arrangement could function at Ust-Luga, I had no prejudice in favour of either perspective. I understood the value of both, and also I had seen for myself how well they could work in tandem, and what could be achieved when they did so. My instinct, which was supported by the advice we received from experts, was that a similar balance between the best aspects of the private and public spheres was the most effective model for Russian Railways to adopt, and this is the case that I made to the President in the course of the lengthy debates that followed.

The reform package that was finally agreed upon, which would unfold over three discrete phases, was distinctly different to the approaches taken by other nations. Although there was substantial provision for competition, to be introduced through partial privatisation of Russian Railways and some of its enterprises, we retained our monopoly on infrastructure, locomotives, operational systems and the majority of the freight businesses. Funding was supposed to come from the profits of our own business activities, a mixture of federal and regional bodies, and the private sector. It was a programme that we believed represented a realistic reflection of Russia's very particular needs: it would simultaneously allow the company to solicit substantial private investment (which was essential for the rejuvenation of the rolling stock), while continuing to provide many of the universal benefits of a state service (for instance, maintaining the network of rail lines that serviced even the most remote corners of the country). Ultimately, what we wanted was to create a new structure, which would support the railways' re-emergence as a dynamic element within Russia's economy.

One priority was changing the corporate culture – to manage as effectively as possible the transition from government institution to a market-orientated company and to ensure that 'best practice' was at the heart of everything we did, which also meant educating everybody involved as to exactly what this term meant; even in 2005 many of its precepts were almost completely unknown in Russia. (I knew that I as CEO had just as much to learn about these theories as even the most junior regional managers.) This was a substantial challenge at the best of times, but even more so in an institution as drenched in tradition and pride as Russian Railways. The esprit de corps of its long-serving employees was so entrenched that it could at times shade into a somewhat conservative mentality, one that left them suspicious of the kind of change that they worried might alter their working lives almost overnight. This led to huge tensions, and rumours quickly began to proliferate. People were concerned that they would lose their jobs, or that their salaries would be slashed. More than that, in an institution where it was not uncommon for sons and daughters to follow in the footsteps of their parents, many were afraid that generations' worth of achievements would be torn up in the name of what they saw as a dubious kind of progress.

Drawing on the advice we sought from foreign consultants, as well as business leaders such as Hartmut Mehdorn, the head of Deutsche Bahn, we did all we could to promote an atmosphere of transparency and fairness. Audit committees became a key part of the way we functioned, and we introduced systems and structures that meant we could trace exactly how every rouble we received was spent. For almost the first time it was possible to identify which departments within the company were losing money. We also looked at the way power was applied within the company. Previous leaders of the railways may have ruled by diktat, imposing change from above and expecting their employees to obey without question, but although we wanted to preserve a strong sense of authority within the organisation, we also understood that the people who worked at Russian Railways deserved to be more involved in the discussions surrounding reforms. The reforms would, after all, have a direct impact on their working lives. We wanted to build a sense of trust that would extend throughout the company.

This attitude would come to be of particular use during the 2008 financial crisis. We had already taken a number of steps to try and insulate our company from the worst effects of the crash, but inevitably there was only so much we could do. We had to acknowledge that the promises of pay rises we had made previously were no longer tenable, and we knew we would be unable to escape a confrontation with the company's trade unions – which was fair enough; we had made these commitments, and I did not want our employees to think that we were making active attempts to escape them. However, faced by a global catastrophe, it was also clear that we had to make hard decisions; we simply did not have enough money.

Since the trade unions within Russian Railways were a strong element in these negotiations, I knew it was essential to talk to them. I began by talking to their leader, pleading with him to assent to a freeze on the increase in wages. But he remained steadfast. It was my responsibility, he reminded me; the board at Russian Railways had made those promises, and they would have to abide by them. Since we were unable to reach a conclusion, I decided to address the workers directly. Along with my staff in the personnel department, I encouraged employees from across the country to appoint representatives – there ended up being around 300 of them – to come to Moscow to discuss these issues. Flanked by my colleagues in the company's senior management, we made our appeal. I remember how one man, a locomotive driver, asked me if, when things picked up, we would be willing to revisit our earlier commitments and ensure that nobody would miss out as a result of the delay. I assured him that we would use half of every single extra rouble the company earned to reimburse those who had lost out. And I am pleased to say that I returned every penny that I promised; it was no more than they deserved.

Alongside changing the nature of the interactions between the management and the workers, we also prioritised education as a means of introducing the right kind of corporate culture. As we had right throughout the modernisation process, we did everything we could to make sure that everyone involved had the best information possible at their fingertips. So once again, we brought in consultants; we entered into a collaboration with the Stockholm Business School; we produced articles; and we offered management courses which were taught at the corporate university we established.

But all this would have been in vain if the board of directors was not also the supreme ruling body within the company. Of course, 100 per cent of our shares were owned by the state, but the idea that, for instance, deputy ministers might sit on the board – as was suggested in some quarters – was something we considered to be intolerable.[17] I knew from my own experience that deputy ministers (in Russia at least) do not exist independently of the ministers they report to. Any deputy minister on our board would inevitably be operating on the orders of their superiors, each of whom would have their own priorities, and a vested interest in making sure that Russian Railways fell into line with them. This could only lead to mess and confusion, as well as undermining our authority and compromising our strategic vision. Instead, we looked to invite respected independent figures – like Mr Mehdorn, who is still on the company's board, or Professor Richard Werner of the European Central Bank Shadow Council – so that they could bring their experience of executive autonomy, and all the lessons that came with it.

Our reforms were also designed to introduce greater accountability. The old ministry had been constantly in debt, but in its new incarnation it was by statute no longer acceptable for it to remain in deficit for more than three years. If this situation persisted, then the new legislation stated that the company would be shrunk, or its share capital reduced, or in the most severe circumstances it could even be closed. The president of the

---

17 This is I think a useful illustration of how far things had changed since I myself had been a deputy minister who sat on a number of corporate boards. At that time, when concepts such as best practice had not really entered the lexicon of Russia's business world, nobody, including myself, thought that there was anything contentious about a minister also occupying influential positions in a private company.

company, together with the chief accountant, was legally bound by the criminal court to be responsible for financial data they provided to the state. Where before, a minister could consider his department to be almost like a small empire in which they were able to exert total control, the new CEO was now required to refer all major decisions to the board of directors for approval.

This was allied with an extensive obligation to answer to the government for everything we did. Because it was part of the strategic plan of the state – and a matter in which the President took a close personal interest – it was considered essential that the government continued to oversee it. Every plan we created, every decision we wanted to make, almost every breath we took, was recorded and analysed and submitted to Moscow.

Another thing that was plain was that Russian Railways could no longer be run as one undivided entity, an approach that may have been practical thirty years previously, but which was no longer sustainable in the twenty-first century. The finances, record-keeping and inventories of all the various elements of the organisation were bundled up together, and this made it almost impossible to measure anything within the organisation, to know which elements were performing well and which needed help or intervention. So, although the parent company remained a majority shareholder, Russian Railways' manifold functions were hived off into 150 daughter companies, each a separate, self-sufficient business with its own budget and board of directors. We were moving away from being run as a national monopoly towards creating a competitive market and ultimately, we hoped, driving up efficiency, and driving down costs.

The changes we began to implement throughout the railway

system eventually allowed us to attract more than $50 billion of private investment. One of the most immediate uses to which we could put this was the renewal of our locomotives and rolling stock – over the course of ten years, we were able to plough in 16 billion roubles into this area. When I joined Russian Railways, we were purchasing forty locomotives a year, but before long that figure had risen to 800. We bought the best models available and did everything we could to increase passenger comfort both within the carriages themselves and at stations (in stark contrast to the Soviet era, where little or no attention was paid to the passengers' welfare).

We also realised that if we purchased the majority of our assets – whether steel for tracks or the locomotives themselves – from domestic manufacturers, we would be able to play a part in stimulating industrial development in the country. We soon became involved in borrowing the most advanced technology available from abroad, or entering into partnerships with foreign firms such as Siemens and setting up everything from metallurgical plants to factories that could produce passenger wagons.

Significant as these changes were, they were also often largely invisible to the public. It was important, we believed, that people should judge the reforms we were implementing not by abstract concepts such as tonnage or profit, which would have meant nothing to them and done even less to improve their lives, but by the quality of their own individual experiences. In partnership with the local authorities, in Moscow we developed a comprehensive plan that ensured the railways that ran around the city became an essential part of the capital's transport system. Alongside this, we built badly needed rail connections to Moscow's major airports and did the same in a number of other Russian cities, notably Kazan.

We also created a high-speed railway from Moscow to St Petersburg: the Sapsan train. It used to be an overnight journey, but now it could be done in under four hours. While some of the first 'Sapsan' trains were attacked by hooligans hurling stones as they passed through remote villages – they did not realise that it was a service that they could use themselves, and saw it as another example of the modern world's bounty passing them by – before long, families were making trips to their local railway station so they could have their photographs taken beside the brand-new trains.

The Sapsan was not Russian Railways' only achievement during these years, but in its ability to make a tangible difference to ordinary people's lives while also providing a spur to the local and national economies, it was an exemplar of the kind of investment-led business model that I believe is the best for Russia. If we had not adopted this approach during the first years of my time at Russian Railways, we would not have been able to undertake projects as vast and expensive as creating much of the transport infrastructure for the Sochi Olympics, building the Severomuysky Tunnel and embarking on the complete renovation of the Trans-Siberian and BAM lines.

However, by 2013 everything had changed. Russia was struggling to cope with economic problems more severe than at any point since the 2008 financial crisis, GDP growth had all but come to a halt, and the word recession was on everyone's lips.

More troublingly, even after the symptoms were beginning to

take their toll, we could not at first determine what was causing them. Ministers suggested it was due to the effects of the global slowdown, whereas a number of bankers argued that it was because big, state-funded infrastructure projects were coming to an end and private companies had not stepped in to keep spending. And we were told by Western economists that it was the result of fundamental structural weaknesses: our overreliance on oil; the overenergetic role of the state in the economy. One thing was clear, though: when a problem is difficult to diagnose, and when it proves impossible to reach any consensus on what caused it, finding a solution becomes even harder.

The situation was exacerbated later that year by the fallout from the conflict in Ukraine, which led to sanctions on long-term borrowing, and also a steep drop in the price of oil. This, combined with the lavish social subsidies and social welfare that Vladimir Putin had promised as part of his 2012 re-election campaign, forced Russia into budget revision.

We could not avoid recognising the bruising new status quo: the state no longer possessed the financial muscle to support investment-based economic growth and, more than that, the political winds had changed. Russia's government had embraced an economic philosophy with which I had little sympathy, and which I knew would in turn be equally unfriendly towards the kind of business model I had become accustomed to following at Russian Railways.

The first blow landed on 11 September 2013, when the Minister for Economic Development, Alexey Ulyukaev, acting with the approval of the President, announced a one-year freeze on the tariffs we were able to charge companies for transporting goods. January 2014 would be the first time in fourteen years that we would be unable to raise prices in the new year. Though the tariff would be increased the following January, it would only be in line with 2014 levels of inflation.

It was a move that slashed Russian Railways' principal source of raising money. To understand the true scale of this decision's consequences, I feel it would be worth spending a moment explaining what tariffs are, and the place they occupy within the Russian economy.

Tariffs are prices charged for state-regulated services, which in Russia have always included what we call our natural monopolies, such as gas, electricity and the railways. They are the only serious mechanism the railway system, which has for more than a century been the sole provider of transport for freight over large parts of the country, can employ to generate income.

The level of control that our government exerts over the whole process is far in excess of what you might find in Western Europe or North America, where, because of increased internal competition and the fact that the tariffs are generally designed to cover only infrastructure costs rather than investment activity, the state is rarely, if ever, involved. The tariff system played a significant role in the Soviet Union's planned economy, as a means of controlling prices, and even after 1991, it was still regularly used to balance or encourage economic development. This might have taken the form of promoting growth in remote parts of the country, helping industries in financial difficulty, or even providing lower tariffs to some neighbouring countries.

It was a reminder, as if one were needed, that there is no such thing as pure, unadulterated free-market capitalism anywhere in the world. The state always plays a role. This might be a question of keeping a car plant or a steel works open that would otherwise be doomed if left to fend for itself. Someone in the government decides that the social or political cost of allowing it to close is too great.

The same is true in Russia. One could, for instance, make an argument to say that the coal industry in Russia has no real right to exist any more. It is a low-value commodity, which also happens to be extremely bulky, so if you were to apply the same tonnage pricing as you do to oil, but factored in the costs involved in mining it in Central Siberia and shifting it to the port of St Petersburg, it is by most metrics insupportable. And yet coal is also the largest employer in Central Siberia, so if you were to shut down the mines there, then the consequences for the regional economy and society would be cataclysmic.

It is another example of the way in which a combination of Russia's size and history have dictated that its transport infrastructure is both unusual in kind, and unusual in complexity. The railways are not just a means of transporting goods from A to B, but are, rather, a three-dimensional economic instrument.

Even before the freeze, the tariffs we were allowed to charge had been too low to be economically prudent (at least as far as we were concerned, others benefited from our reduced prices). But what became clear in 2013 was that a decision had been made that other players in this intricate system were going to be privileged at our expense. While we were expected to somehow find a way of accommodating the devastating impact of the tariff freeze, no similar retrenchment had been asked of the coal and other industries. The savings we were being asked to find were being used to subsidise private enterprises that had evaded the squeeze altogether.

I am not economically illiterate; I could see the rationale behind this decision. With its rate of GDP growth falling, Russia had effectively entered into recession. Freezing tariffs was an attempt to reduce inflation and provide a spur to the economy. By reducing the cost of doing business, the cost of goods could be kept in check, something that it was hoped would put a bit more money into the pockets of consumers. At a time when concern was rising among the general public about the cost of living, and in the context of a presidency that had begun with protestors on the streets, this move also made a certain amount of political sense.

Personally though, I do not believe that taking an axe to spending is the right way to deal with a recession. For one thing, there was no guarantee at all that the private businesses that stood to benefit would necessarily invest the money back into the economy; they were just as likely to either keep it on their balance sheets, or decide to invest it in more stable markets abroad. I have lived long enough to know that private enterprises will always be guided by their own bottom line; they cannot be expected to tailor their strategy to suit the nation's interests alone.

I believe a national problem demands national direction. I have always liked the example given by Wassily Leontief, the Russian-born Nobel Prize laureate, who used to say that the economy is like a yacht. If there is no wind, or ability to accrue profit, then the yacht will remain still. However, if the state does not provide a figurative map and compass to guide the yacht, the economy is bound to go in the wrong direction. The economy of the former USSR had lost all the wind from its sails, so it ended up becalmed. By contrast, one could argue that today the American economy has no direction. Neither of these is sustainable – there has to be a balance between private entrepreneurship and state control in order for the yacht to sail smoothly.

My own response to the recession would have been to pursue a programme of reindustrialisation. By embarking on large-scale state-funded infrastructure projects, creating an environment that would have encouraged entrepreneurs to invest, or providing tax incentives that offered private companies joint-financing to enable them to renew fixed assets in important industries, we would have been able to stimulate demand, reinvigorate our industrial base and give the economy the kick-start it needed.

Russian Railways was a case in point. Our operations contributed 1.7 per cent to Russia's GDP in 2013; cutting the tariffs would only prejudice our chances of improving on or even matching this figure in subsequent years, and would have a malign effect on many other elements with the country. (By this stage, our manufacturing and infrastructure creation programmes had direct links to at least nineteen other sectors of the economy; if our ability to spend was restricted, then there would also be an impact on industrial enterprises throughout Russia.)

But nobody seemed to be listening to our arguments. In fact, it was around this time that the suggestion started to be made that, irrespective of the financial situation, the natural monopolies that were the victims of the tariff freeze were inefficient anyway and would all benefit from a spell of cost-cutting. Certain people began to mutter that we had had things easy for too long, that we had become accustomed to the good life, that we were just sucking up public money.

This, as much as anything else, convinced me that the whole policy was a purely emotional, political decision. We were, for instance, the only state-owned company, maybe even the only company in Russia, which was year on year increasing our efficiency by 10 per cent. The first deputy Prime Minister Igor Shuvalov had declared us the most efficient state-owned company. And yet here we were again, playing the role that the railways have had to assume so many times before: the scapegoat. (The railways have always been a convenient target for those looking for someone, or something, to blame. In the days of the Soviet Union, for example, party apparatchiks would always blame railway representatives when deliveries of fertilisers fell, wilfully ignoring the cyclical nature of the fertiliser industry.) The value we created was being cannibalised to subsidise the operations of private companies, and yet we were still being accused of inefficiency, or worse.

In one fell swoop, we would be going from a profit-making enterprise to one looking at a 90-billion-rouble loss on its balance sheet. One stinging consequence of all of this – something else that had not been anticipated by the policy-makers – was that while in the past we had had great success both in collaborating with foreign enterprises such as Siemans and Talgo, and with the Western financial system (by selling our bonds on the global market), the freezing of the tariffs made us less attractive to overseas investors almost overnight.

We argued fiercely, but without success, for the right to be able to introduce variable tariffs that would have allowed us to respond nimbly to changes in market conditions. If the price of coal went up, we would raise our tariffs accordingly. And, similarly, we could react to a drop in commodity prices by reducing our tariffs. Since Russian Railways is not the only cargo operator in Russia, our competitors (who are not owned by the state and thus have far greater leeway when it comes to setting their tariffs) could undercut us when prices were low. The arrangement that was foisted on us in 2013 represented the worst of both worlds, not least because, unlike the other cargo companies, we still bore a lot of the cost for maintaining and repairing the infrastructure.

As a last resort, in October 2013 we made an approach to the Ministry of Finance for extra subsidies, which we hoped to use to mitigate as far as possible the impact of the tariff freeze and allow us to maintain our investment programme. It was firmly rebuffed. We had made this move more in hope than expectation, but the definitiveness of the ministry's response – the confirmation it brought that our chances of raising the money we so desperately needed had receded to an infinitesimally small point – was another crushing blow. (I have noted with some interest that my intuition then has been proved correct now, and the government, aware that it is unable to secure the income it needs from elsewhere, is using its reserves to invest in infrastructure programmes. This has not led, as I was warned it would, to increased inflation – quite the opposite, in fact.)

The tariff freeze brought to an end the expansive period in which we had embarked successfully on great projects such as Sochi and the modernisation of the Transsib and BAM lines. As 2014 rolled around, the impact of the cost-cutting began to make itself felt with ever greater force. Repairs and maintenance soaked up what money we had and I learned that there is little so dispiriting for a

CEO as watching your company's assets depreciate in value and to be unable to make the investments needed to arrest the slide. With any kind of state support now a distant memory, and our income slashed as a result of the tariff freeze, it was clear that nobody was interested any more in how the railways could be used to stimulate economic growth; the focus was on how much money could be saved. 'Opex optimisation' had become the order of the day.

From then on, we were told to make ever-greater efficiency savings. People began circling around Russian Railways like vultures. They demanded additional divestments of our 'non-core assets' (such as Greek ports) and activities such as hospitals, hotels and schools. Some of these cuts could be made relatively easily, but at other times it could feel as if we were being asked to pick apart the intricate, interdependent railway system by people who did not realise the implications of doing so. Almost a decade previously, as we embarked on the reform of Russian Railways, the President had warned me against making irrevocable mistakes; I feared that in the harsh new world into which our politics had stepped, they would soon become unavoidable.

What value could accrue from slicing away hospitals that were integral parts of local communities – sometimes providing the only medical care for miles around – and which also had a measurable impact on the performance of Russian Railways? For instance, when Russia was struck by an influenza epidemic, our employees fell sick at a rate of 18 per cent less than the country's average. Was it really going to be more efficient to sell this part of our holdings off?

We often resisted some of the savings that people tried to force upon us, and often we were successful. But it was symptomatic of an erosion of vision, the effects of which you could see at the very top levels of the government too. My life up until this point had always been filled with argument and discussion with the people around me, be they friends, politicians or business associates. I, like them, have been eager to debate every aspect of our country's economic, social and political evolution in the years since 1991. I remember, for instance, how many of us disagreed with Vladimir Putin over whether Leningrad should revert its name to St Petersburg or Petrograd (named after Peter the Great; Petersburg was hastily changed to the less German-sounding Petrograd in 1914). The referendum of June 1991, in which the city's population voted for St Petersburg (and at the same time elected Anatoly Sobchak as mayor), settled this issue, but there would be plenty of others for us to debate in the years that followed.

I remember endless fierce exchanges about the role of the state, about foreign policy, about how far reform should be pursued – anything that touched on the kind of nation we thought Russia should be aiming to become. And these disputes had spilled into our deliberations about the modernisation of Russia's railway system.

But now, the free-marketeers with whom I had once argued so forcefully had all lost their seats at the government's top table.[18]

---

18 I remember having an argument in Moscow with Alexey Kudrin about the extent to which state intervention in the economy should be limited or not (an argument that remains as vital as ever). Later on, after he became Minister of Finance, he told me, 'stop arguing with me, I am a professor and I give lectures on this subject'. This did not end the argument; far from it. Rather, it was a spur for me to acquire a PhD in Political Science and take up a number of academic positions, including as Head of the State Policy Department at Lomonosov Moscow State University, and as a visiting professor at Peking University and the Stockholm School of Economics. So I am grateful for those words, which I imagine he has not given a moment's consideration since, because they have opened up another rewarding dimension in my life (and in the process provided yet another example of the law of unintended consequences in action). We are still no closer to reaching an agreement about the role the state should play in civil society, but it is worth remembering that after he was ousted from his position in 2011, I was the first to extend a hand of support to him.

Kudrin was no longer part of the government, Gref was running a bank, Chubais an investment fund. The men who had stepped into their places were low-profile bureaucrats. They were perfectly competent when it came to supplying ad-hoc solutions to the problems that were thrust beneath their noses, but unable or unwilling to lift their heads and try to work out what kind of direction they should be steering the country in so that it might avoid those issues in the future.

What made all of this increasingly hard for me to bear was that it was coupled with more pronounced efforts by the government to exercise control over Russian Railways from the inside. This process had begun as early as 2008, when there was a substantial turnover in government personnel. Because we were a state-owned company, the government had the authority to construct the board of directors. They exercised this right by appointing young entrepreneurs who had little experience of the real world (and even less knowledge of transport systems) into senior roles. The government knew that in doing this they would not only be able to circumscribe the authority of the company's management, but also to gain an upper hand in the decision-making process. It felt as if they were trying, step by step, to change the DNA of the organisation and undermine all the efforts we had made to create a distinct and robust corporate culture.

Russian Railways was a huge company employing over a million people, whose operations exerted a monumental influence on the country's economic and social life. The board had always been populated by highly respected railway professionals with many years of service in the field; it deserved more than boys who it seemed had only just escaped adolescence sitting in sullen silence when questions they did not understand were raised in board meetings.

The government – or to be more precise, certain elements within it – began to intervene more and more regularly into the operations of the company. The state parachuted in its own 'independent experts', but even a cursory glance at a list of those people who were imposed upon us would tell you that, in contrast to the existing members of the board, these new faces were not professionals in the field; they possessed no obvious expertise, and it was as if they were randomly chosen.

With them came a special independent governmental group who, I learned, were empowered to scrutinise our investment programmes. They had the right to criticise our budget and recommend drastic changes to it. Of course, I had no objection to oversight, and I welcomed any input from experts that promised to help improve our performance – why else would we have spent so much money on the services provided by research institutes and consultancy firms? – but it was difficult to discern anything constructive in the role this group was playing. We were manoeuvred into spending hundreds of hours in discussions with environmental, financial and law-enforcement agencies. They asked endless questions and demanded we provided them with colossal quantities of documentation to support our replies. It got to the point where we had to hire a lorry to deliver the paperwork they claimed was so essential. With hindsight it is clear that all this paper-shuffling was a cleverly implemented plan designed to use endless foot-dragging bureaucracy to smother any attempt we made to embark on large-scale capital expenditure.

In 2011, Alexander Zhukov was succeeded as chairman of the

board of directors by Kirill Androsov. Mr Zhukov was a flinty, sometimes unbending figure with whom I had numerous arguments about the company's strategy, but he was always adamant that the board should not interfere with the technical aspects of the work of Russian Railways. The arrival of Mr Androsov, by contrast, signalled a profound and disruptive realignment of the relationship between the management and the board of directors, as well as of the company's balance of power. His allies in the Finance and Economic Development ministries tried to insist that Androsov alone should be in direct contact with the state, and that Androsov alone should be responsible for implementing its decisions, even though the ultimate responsibility for their results still rested on the shoulders of the CEO and his management team. Androsov was followed in 2015 by Arkady Dvorkovich. Deliberately or not, it was clear to me that the balance of power in the company had shifted, and it was no longer able to operate in the way that I believed was most efficient.

For a long time the extension of high-speed railway lines, such as the Sapsan, which had been such a success in linking Moscow and St Petersburg to other regions of Russia, had been a subject about which I was incredibly passionate. I had become accustomed to thinking that, with Sochi behind me, I would stay on long enough to see through their introduction before retiring. This was, in fact, what I had told the President himself when some time previously he had asked me about extending my contract. And yet, by 2015 it was painfully evident that the conditions to achieve this no longer existed, and that even though I was still CEO of Russian Railways in name, in practice I now only wielded a fraction of the power that I'd had a decade previously. So the reasons behind my departure from RZD are more complex, and at the same time more mundane in comparison to the speculations my decision triggered. I was no different to any other employee in any other organisation: I knew that I was no longer the right man for the job.

I was not born a number cruncher; I do not possess the kind of personality that was made to deliver profits by slashing costs. I am more suited to creating things out of nothing, like Ust-Luga, the Sapsan trains, or the roads and railways that made the Sochi Olympics possible. I had flourished in the years when Russia had invested in its economy and infrastructure. When that model changed, when it seemed as if anybody else with any kind of vision had left the political stage, I realised, though it hurt me to do so, that I could not change with it. It was time to go.

CHAPTER EIGHT

CRUEL AND
TWISTED ROADS

How long, I asked myself, was this going to last? The euphoria of having got Jon Kil Su, the North Korean Minister of Railways, and Kang Kyung Ho, the president of the South Korean railway company Korail, in a room together – for the first time since the war had torn the two nations irrevocably apart fifty years ago – had swiftly given way to frustration as it became clear that neither side was willing to talk. Though I knew that in North Korea contact with South Koreans was prohibited, this felt ridiculous. It was March 2006 and we were supposed to be discussing the development of the Trans-Korean Railway, a project that promised to not only ease the crippling tensions in this fractious peninsula, but also to bring substantial economic benefits in its wake. (I was as keen as anyone to do whatever I could to help support the decisions taken by our respective leaders. However, ultimately, Russian Railways was not in the business of paying for politics.) A conference in Vladivostok had ended without either party shaking hands or even looking at each other, so I invited each set of representatives to Irkutsk to visit Lake Baikal. I hoped that time spent beside the 'world's reservoir', might help lead to a breakthrough. My hopes were dashed almost immediately. Lengthy conversations – filtered laboriously through interpreters – went nowhere. I began to think that all of the effort I had put into even getting them into the same room would turn out to be a huge waste of time. Seconds became minutes, minutes became hours, mealtimes came and went, and, still, we could make no progress.

The day's meeting came to an end and we moved on to dinner. Wanting to salvage something, I was anxious to get a memo signed by all three sides that would at the very least stand as a document of our shared intentions. I had no more luck with this – it soon became clear that the North Koreans did not have the authority to endorse it. I felt lost. It seemed to me that I had exhausted all possibility of breaking the ice, but I had not count-ed on what happened next. I whispered to the wife of the Korail president, who was sitting next to me, 'This is unbelievable, a disaster.' Immediately she replied: 'Give me the right to make the next toast.' What did I have to lose?[19]

She stood up and began by making a handful of polite pre-liminary phrases, before turning to Jon Kil Su and addressing him directly. It was as if a bolt of lightning had struck the room; we all sat stunned, waiting for her next words. 'Distinguished

---

19 The president's wife was a highly cultured, cosmopolitan woman, and in retrospect perhaps I should not have been surprised by the elegant and daring solution she devised. In Korea, she owned a successful animation studio that translated American cartoons, and her husband had been a dissident under the country's former dictator, Park Chung-hee. In fact, his opposition had earned him a death sentence, and only the revelation that a number of years earlier, when he had been a teacher, he had saved Park's boy from a beating at the hands of other children, ensured he would be spared a grim visit to the executioner.

minister,' she said, and what could he do other than meet her gaze? 'In Korean tradition, an older person is considered like an older brother for the younger people with him. We are talking about serious things with great value for our societies. Please permit me to address you as an older brother. As an older brother I would like to suggest that we drink to the success of this project.' We all emptied our glasses. 'As an older brother,' she continued, 'I would like to shake your hand.'

Afterwards the North Korean railway minister came to me, his face still showing the effects of the surprise we had all experienced a few moments earlier. 'Listen, the fact that I've shaken the hand of a South Korean is already a very severe mistake, perhaps illegal. Don't ask me to sign the memo, but there is a way. You, as chairman, could sign the memo alone. If I add my signature, I will be thrown into jail.' To my great relief Kang Kyung Ho agreed. I left that evening clutching the memo as if it were written in gold. I knew how close the meetings had come to abject failure; it was a reminder, if one were needed, of the havoc that intransigent government policy can wreak on even the simplest of human exchanges. More lessons like this would follow during my career at Russian Railways, including a horrific, bloody incident that demonstrated to me how cruel and twisted are the roads down which ideology can lead a man.

Russian Railways employs a number of men who always sleep with what we called their 'emergency luggage' beside their beds. This bag contains underwear, socks, a few cans of food, a bottle of strong alcohol, razors and a toothbrush. As soon as they learn of an emergency these men grab their luggage and rush out, whatever the weather, often not knowing where they are going, or how long they will be away for.

I thought of them that terrible night, 27 November 2009, when I was first told that there had been an incident involving the Nevsky Express, the train that runs between Moscow and St Petersburg. Unlike them I was not dragged from my bed. I had in fact been sitting in a dinner jacket and black tie at the Mariinsky Opera Theatre in St Petersburg, with my wife by my side; how strange and uncomfortable to receive such macabre news in surroundings like that.

I learned that a train had been derailed by a bomb, that there had been numerous casualties, though nobody knew exactly how many, and that there was nobody with real authority on hand at the site itself. The gruesome air of unreality that descended as I tried to digest the scattered pieces of information I was given soon gave way to something more practical: I found that my thoughts had begun to work like a well-oiled machine and that I knew exactly what needed to be done. I immediately called the head of October Railway, the section of Russian Railways responsible for this line, and ordered that a special train should be arranged so I could travel to the scene of the tragedy – which was over 200 miles away near the town of Bologoye – as quickly as possible. Next I began to make arrangements for a group to follow on my heels. I also sent someone to find a set of clothes more suited to the occasion than the formal suit in which I was currently encased.

Within an hour the locomotive and a couple of wagons were ready and we sped through the dark – a journey of two and a half hours in which we continued to desperately try and find out as much information as possible.

I will never forget the scenes that confronted me as I stepped off the train. Powerful lamps had been rigged up around the perimeter to shed light on the carnage below. A big crater had been gouged out of the ground, haloed by hideously twisted strips of track. Next to it, four carriages lay on their sides, surrounded by yet more debris and bodies covered by blankets – I shiver to think what horrors these concealed.

Almost the first person I saw was a man I knew from St Petersburg, who stumbled towards me, his face covered in blood. I had already been informed that some of my friends were among the more than 653 passengers and twenty-nine staff – the train was full – and now this guy, with his cheeks and brow streaked with crimson, was telling me that a mutual acquaintance had been killed. They had been at the front of their carriage, which in the space of a second, or so it seemed, had been transformed into a grotesque wasteland of smoke and stone. One survived, the other's life had been extinguished.

My interlocutor seemed dazed still – hardly surprising under the circumstances – and I urged him to seek medical attention for his bleeding. He shook his head: 'No, no, no, Vladimir Ivanovich, I will stay with my friend here.' His was the first display of dignity and courage I witnessed that night, and it would not be the last.

I eventually ordered him to put himself in the care of the medical team who had set up their equipment a little distance away, and watched as he picked his way past the shattered train towards them. Everywhere I looked people wandered around, their eyes still wild and stunned; even the policemen there seemed unable to determine what they should be doing. It was essential that some degree of organisation should be brought to the situation as soon as possible.

At no point in my career had I ever been in a position like this before. What in anyone's life could prepare them to witness such horror? But I was the most senior figure on the ground, and I knew it was my responsibility to take control. We found a small chamber that had been used by Russian Railways to house electrical equipment and, together with representatives from Russian Railways, the local police and the FSB, I squeezed in to our makeshift incident room. I turned to them and said, 'I know I am only a railwayman, so perhaps I have no right to give you orders, but you know who I am, you know my history and you all know too that we will be unable to achieve anything here unless we cooperate.' With that, we got to work.

Our first priorities were to secure the perimeter (there would be no good in trying to save lives if terrorists were able to creep back and wreak more havoc), help the injured, recover those corpses that had not already been lifted from the wreckage, and restore what infrastructure we could so that traffic between the two cities could resume. Some of the dead had been buried so deep in the ground in the blast that it was two or three days before the special equipment necessary to excavate them was available, and, anyway, we were not yet permitted to start this kind of work – we could not risk contaminating the crime scene before investigators from the FSB arrived to take prints and subject the wreckage to a forensic examination. Still, knowing that we were close to so much torn flesh was a terrible, ghoulish feeling.

Over the course of those first few hours, we dragged as many survivors as we could to safety. The next day, those who were capable were interviewed by the Investigative Committee led by Alexander Bastrykin, who had arrived to try to build up an accurate picture of what exactly had happened. As Bastrykin and his men continued their search for clues, I remained in charge of the rescue operation. (I learned the next morning that the Minister of Transport at that time, Igor Levitin, together with Sergey Shoygu, the head of the Ministry of Emergency Situations, approached the President, requesting his permission to leave Moscow and hurry to the scene. 'And who is now organising the work there?' the President asked. When he learned it was me he said, 'Listen, if Yakunin is there, you don't need to go; he will do everything you can. Talk to him, give him any assistance he needs, but leave him in charge.')

Nobody slept – how could they when there was so much to do? – and by the next morning we had restored what organisation we could to the shattered stretch of railway line. Workers from the Ministry of Emergency Situations had restored lines of communication, including video communication, which meant that we were able to make a first report on the situation to the President. A little later, just as I sat down for a moment's rest at a table in a special wagon that we had temporarily converted into a kind of kitchen, I heard a loud explosion – another bomb, left there in a cowardly attempt to injure or kill the rescue workers, had detonated, triggered remotely by a terrorist's mobile phone. I rushed to the source of the noise, where I found that only Bastrykin had suffered any kind of wound, from gravel thrown into the air by the blast. He would be hospitalised, but his injuries were not serious. My overwhelming feeling was relief; the tragedy would eventually take twenty-eight lives, but his would not be among them.

At times like this, when confronted by evidence of such wickedness, it is easy to feel one's faith in man's essential goodness dwindling. But life has its own ways of restoring your optimism. A few days later one of my colleagues pointed out a nearby house that had been damaged by the accident. I was told that it belonged to 78-year-old former railway worker (she had served for forty years) Elena Golubeva, who despite living in poverty had donated blankets, pillows, everything she had, to help the injured. She could ill afford to lose her possessions like this, but she had not thought twice.

When I learned of her sacrifice, I immediately ordered that we should do everything possible to repair the destruction wrought on her yard. We did not confine ourselves to this; after what she had done there was no way she could be allowed to live any longer in a home as shabby as hers had been. Workers from Russian Railways built her a new home, complete with toilet and bath, and even connecting her residence to the electricity network. Unbelievably, it was the first time she had had access to it.

Her actions had not gone unobserved by the President. During the course of our first telephone conversation after my return to Moscow, Mr Putin asked me if I was ready and willing to help this lady. My first reaction was pride that her generosity of spirit had got his attention, and I was proud too to be able to tell him that we had already met his expectations. Not only had we built for her a modern new home, but our management council ensured she received the most prestigious decoration we could bestow upon her.

More information emerged over the weeks following the tragedy. On the one hand, it was satisfying to be able to celebrate the heroism of men like the driver and his assistant, whose quick-thinking and cool nerves as they struggled to control their devastated train ensured that more lives were not lost. On the other, I was disgusted to watch rumours spread that sought to pin the blame for elements of the tragedy on either Russian Railways or the companies that built our equipment. As soon as news of the accident emerged, allegations were made on the Internet that Russian Railways was involved in some kind of conspiracy. They claimed that there had been no terrorist attack; we had just failed in our maintenance. It was suggested that the carriages were defective, or that the seats had not been attached to the floor with sufficient care. There was no truth in either smear, but nevertheless the bad feelings they created still linger; the stains caused by lies are hard to wash away. I did not know it then, but this represented the beginning of a campaign of information warfare against Russian Railways, and me personally, that continues to be waged to this day.

In time we learned that the derailment was in all likelihood the handiwork of fanatics operating on the orders of the separatist Chechen leader Dokka Umarov, an Islamist who had not long before proclaimed himself Emir of the entire North Caucasus region. The Nevsky Express was yet another in the long sequence of atrocities inflicted on the Russian people by terrorists with a range of agendas, dating back to the chaos of the Yeltsin era. Since well before 9/11, we have struggled with this threat, often fighting men who had been armed and funded by the very Western powers who would be sent into panic by the assault on New York's Twin Towers. Beslan, Nord-Ost, the Domodedovo airport bombing, the repeated bombings of the Moscow Metro, and several others, each marked a devastating page in Russia's recent history.[20]

The tragedy of the Nevsky Express hurt me deeply. I found that everything changes once you have been confronted with the sight of soil stained with blood, and blanket-shrouded corpses lined up in a tidy row. As soon as I was back in Moscow, I introduced to the President and the government a whole raft of new security measures designed to do as much as possible to prevent a tragedy like that from occurring again. CCTV cameras were installed along the length of the St Petersburg to Moscow line, which was to be provided with extra protection by armed guards employed by the Ministry of Transport, and we also built metal detectors into the entrance of each of the capital's stations (a task that the Prime Minister had decreed we should complete in four days, which somehow we managed).

There is, however, much in the world we live in now that is so frightening to me, I believe that no amount of security gates and armed guards would be enough to keep us safe. In fact, I feel more pessimistic about the world now than I did thirty years ago, when the prospect of a nuclear war felt like a live threat.

---

20 The Russian people have, generally speaking at least, supported their government's engagement in Syria because they believe it will make them safer (it is not for them a question, as is sometimes suggested, of Russia flexing its muscles on the world stage once more). The idea of Russian citizens, hardened by experience on Syria's battlefields, returning to wreak havoc in the cities of their own country, fills them, quite understandably, with fear, and they find it difficult to comprehend why Western nations have left the job of policing this failed state to Putin's administration.

In the past decade, science and technology have penetrated our lives in a completely unprecedented, and likely irrevocable, manner. Sometimes this is a wholly good thing, sometimes wholly bad, but usually the newly developed technology contains within it the capacity for both. For instance, while nuclear power is a source of valuable energy, a nuclear bomb – as Nagasaki and Hiroshima proved – has a devastating destructive capacity. A gun is a lump of metal that is only as dangerous as the man holding it, but when one is familiar with the evil of which others are capable, this knowledge does little to reassure.

There is a story told about how, in ancient Rome, a man approached the emperor and told him that he had invented a devastating new weapon that could give his troops an unbelievable advantage. It was very simple, just a long cylinder studded with huge nails that, if suspended between two horses, could cause horrendous casualties. But rather than reward the man, the emperor ordered that he should be immediately arrested and executed before he had the chance to share his idea with anyone else. When the emperor's shocked adviser asked him why he had passed up the opportunity to acquire a weapon of mass destruction, the emperor replied that he could not countenance employing something so inhuman.

I think of this when I read in the press that a new cold war has begun between Russia and the West, even though I am not sure that it ever really came to an end. President George H. W. Bush of the United States may have declared that the conflict had been won by the capitalist powers, but the struggle continued in the shadows. It could be said that a cold-war mentality persists to this day in Russia and the USA alike because the security services, diplomatic corps and civil services of both nations are still staffed by many people who lived through it. While it is easy (sometimes, at least) to reform institutions, it is far harder to reorient people's minds. Certainly it would be naïve to think that in our divided world any country with substantial resources would ever stop its intelligence work, no matter how loyalties are realigned.

The development of technology has only accelerated this aggressive activity, and its potential reach and potency far exceeds anything I ever encountered during my career in the KGB. As a former intelligence officer, I would of course like to be confident that Russia could develop and employ the tools needed to fight back against the machinations of hostile powers, but as a civilian I'm extremely concerned about the complete erosion of privacy that the escalation of this cyber war (and what else could you call it?) would entail – that every email, every telephone call, every text message will be monitored, that information harvested from my conversations is relentlessly piling up somewhere, until such a time as someone deploys it to harm me or my family.

There always used to be a quid pro quo. In both the West and the Soviet Union, citizens exchanged certain rights in return for security. That was the (sometimes unspoken) deal that underpinned the preservation of our respective ways of life. But there was nothing then that could ever compare to the monumental power that now resides in the hands of those who are supposed to be protecting us. The kind of monitoring performed by the CIA and the KGB during the cold war now feels completely obsolete, even innocent; and we are moving towards a disturbing paradox: the more sophisticated the country, the less free the individual. It is a new kind of imperialism in which governments as well as criminals can colonise your private life.

We can now be menaced as we sit in our own homes by anonymous figures we will never even see. The wife of my younger son recently received a letter from a body describing themselves as 'The Association of Hackers'. Its authors pretended that they had somehow got hold of her tax records, alleged that they showed she was guilty of fraud and said that if she would prefer that they didn't publicise this information, then she'd better pay up. It was, of course, complete bullshit. My daughter-in-law, who was unsurprisingly somewhat rattled by this communication, went to see an IT specialist. She told him that she was planning to take the matter to the police. His reply shocked her:

> Forget about it. It would be better to forget everything. You don't pay, you don't enter into any communication, but nor should you approach anyone in law enforcement. There's no point. Nobody knows who they are, or where they are based, and law enforcement won't have the resources to be able to find out.

Who now is willing to show the same self-restraint as that Roman emperor? Our capacity to inflict harm has decisively exceeded our abilities to discern the moral consequences. The dream of unlimited progress has turned sour; it is as if we have forgotten that mankind is, before it is anything else, part of the natural world. Technology has leapt so far ahead of any ethical or legal restraint that the only logical conclusion, if we continue along the same route, is the total dehumanisation of society. Control of the future will be shared by those who possess wealth and cyber power. The rank and file will be involved in a desperate attempt to preserve what is left of their exposed and pillaged privacy.

This technological threat is exacerbated by the proxy war that is being played out in the world's newspapers and television sets. I am privileged enough to be able to watch both the Western and Russian mass media, and I can see how both manipulate their audiences. To my mind, the neo-liberal consensus that still dominates in the US and Europe bears terrifying similarities to the worldview of the Bolsheviks. Like them, it will not allow even a glimpse of anything good on the other, demonised side, and it certainly looks as if our critics abandoned the presumption of innocence a long time ago.

Consider this: when was the last time you read anything positive in your newspaper about Russia or Putin? When was the last time that even activities that fall outside the political sphere, like ballet or science, received any recognition in the Western media? Why does every article about Russia seem to be accompanied by a photograph of its president? If a story appears in the Russian press, or if a Russian official speaks, then it is immediately damned as propaganda. When, in the midst of an international crisis, Russia calls for moderation and negotiations, we are criticised. In those cases where we do employ military force, then the worst possible construction is placed on our every move. Is it any wonder that, with every passing day, my country and the West are drifting further apart?

It can feel sometimes as though people in the West slip almost without thinking into an attitude towards Russia established well over a hundred years ago. Britain's first serious outbreak of

Russophobia came in the late 1870s, but the suspicion of its motives dates to before the Crimean War two decades previously, and I do not feel as if this mindset has ever been shrugged off.

Most people are not interested enough to find out the truth for themselves – instead, they are prey to absurd and dangerous simplifications. If their worldview is based on what they see from watching the television news with half an eye open, or flicking listlessly through the newspapers, then is it any wonder that they believe it when they are told that Putin is a devil?

Not long ago a friend of mine, Václav Klaus, who at the time was the honorary president of a prestigious university in the United States, made a statement highlighting how pervasive anti-Russian propaganda had become. Not long afterwards, the institution suggested, politely but firmly, that it might be a good time for him to resign from his post. That kind of stubbornness, that kind of inability to see beyond walls, to learn, to listen to others, always brings severe consequences in its train, and it fills me with fear.

In 2014, I was, along with a number of Russian officials and businessmen, placed on the US State Department's sanctions list. It decreed that I am forbidden from travelling to the US, that any assets I might have had in the US should be frozen, and that US citizens and corporations are banned from entering into business transactions with me. It seems imposing, but in practice it does not change much; I do very little business in the States. But on a personal level, it has created an uncomfortable new status for me, one that also has ramifications for my family, affecting their lives and plans. It felt as if the sanctions were not used to target genuinely dangerous individuals, but to make a point: we have the ability and, furthermore, we also believe we have the right, to obstruct the lives of anyone we wish. This to my mind has been a grievous mistake, because the only concrete thing they have achieved by trying to turn a small group of Russians into pariahs is to have created an atmosphere of suspicion and suppression in their own society. They are like doctors who have been infected by the virus they were trying to cure; sanctions have introduced a disease into the Western community.

This attitude only serves to make regular Russians believe that the West represents an enemy and that as a result it is time to draw back from the world, consolidate and prepare to fight back. It devastates the chance of conducting any kind of meaningful dialogue. The same is true of the constant personal attacks made on Vladimir Putin. It is no secret that Russians can shoulder a great many burdens, and bear suffering like no other nation on earth, but they will not stand being insulted. They experience an insult to their leader as if it is an insult to them and their country too. (This is a sentiment articulated best by Alexander Pushkin in 1826: 'Of course, I despise my fatherland from head to foot – however, I am annoyed when a foreigner shares this feeling with me.') That is the greatest mistake committed by the leaders in the West. They just do not understand. The more the Russian people feel as if they are being attacked, the fiercer their reaction will be, and that is dangerous.

My life has been enriched by encounters with men and women from other cultures. I have been the recipient of spontaneous gestures of warmth and generosity, and witnessed the very best of human nature, such as the Americans who dropped everything to come to the aid of a crushed city many miles away in Armenia and the elderly former railway worker who gave so many of her possessions up to help those wounded in the attack on the Nevsky Express. None of these people behaved that way because it was their government's policy; in some cases, they were in fact acting contrary to it. I was first elected, unanimously, to be the President of the International Union of Railways (the first ever Russian to occupy this post) in 2012, and reconfirmed two years later. During this period, one of heightened international tension, I never noticed any bad feeling from my peers in that professional community, not even a glimpse of it, towards Russian Railways, or Russia, or the Russian people. I received the vote of the American delegate even though I was the subject of sanctions imposed by his own party.

By contrast, I have also seen how so-called diplomacy can petrify a person's natural inclination to reach out in friendship to others. The exchange I witnessed between the two Koreans exemplifies this officially sponsored degradation of the ability and will to communicate.

I spent enough time working as a diplomat to know that, these days, official channels are a fruitless way of conducting international dialogue, or even meaningful negotiations. There is rarely an attempt to create a mutual basis for understanding, even at a time when, with the international community more fractured and wounded than I have ever seen it, one would imagine that this kind of dialogue between civilisations is sorely needed. Diplomacy has been reduced to an exchange of prepared statements, an attempt at mutual manipulation, and I have come to believe that it requires either a stroke of luck – such as the one delivered by Kang Kyung Ho's wife – or the kind of catastrophe that reminds both parties of their shared humanity – such as the earthquake at Spitak – to break through these barriers.

What is terrifying to me is that, while the world order – where capitalism faced communism – as we once knew it has broken into pieces, nothing has emerged in the time since that is capable of restoring any kind of stability and balance. The West wants to draw a new world map, but it does not recognise that, by doing so, it has created a set of circumstances that is already turning against it. This is partly due to the dubious relationships it has entered into. Nobody would claim that Saudi Arabia is a paragon of democracy or human rights, and yet silence prevails because the country is an important ally of the West. To my mind, that is a very dangerous precedent – a return to the kind of policy encapsulated by the comment Franklin Delano Roosevelt allegedly made about the murderous Dominican dictator Rafael Trujillo: 'He may be a son of a bitch, but he's our son of a bitch.'

I feel a genuine sense of responsibility – to my children, to my grandchildren, to everyone I care for – to try to do what I can to de-escalate the tensions that threaten to plunge our world into chaos, but no matter how strongly one feels, it is hard for a lone voice to make itself heard. Harder still when you know that your arguments will be struck away by people who take one look at you, raise their noses into the air, and say, 'He is Russian, he used to be in the KGB, he used to occupy a high-ranking position in Russia; whatever he is saying is just propaganda bullshit.' This is primitive, and I cannot accept it. I can only hope that one day we will be able to change this attitude.

I cofounded the Dialogue of Civilizations, an independent

NGO, in early 2002. I wanted to help create an independent organisation – one that did not belong to any country, any government, or even any single individual, and which did not have to wait for good fortune or a disaster in order to be able to encourage meaningful communication between nations. It was also, at least in part, a response to Professor Samuel Huntington's influential book *The Clash of Civilizations*, which had been published six years previously. He suggested that increased contact between Western nations and the Islamic world would lead only to increased tension and confrontation. We felt as if we wanted to propose a different kind of programme for the future of human interaction. We wanted to use the Dialogue of Civilizations as an instrument to replace the harsh words that have become diplomacy's currency, to replace conflict with conversation.

Too much is made of difference, and not enough of the many values we share. It is bizarre that people draw a fault line between Orthodoxy and the other Christian confessions, when in fact they have far greater cause to be united than divided. That is the emphasis we wanted to find in the Dialogue of Civilizations: communication founded on what we have in common rather than on what sets us apart.

Our aim is that every civilisation, whether large or small, is represented, and that they should all have an equal voice. Although we aim to identify and foster common values, we know that standardisation is not possible, nor is it desirable. We know that it is important to view world events without prejudice and to acknowledge that we are different: we have different cultures, different histories, different tastes. This is why I cannot accept the term 'universal values'. (Who gets to set them? Who should police them?) Human diversity is something we should celebrate if the aggressive propaganda that seeks to set neighbour against neighbour is to be resisted.

The people with whom I created the Dialogue of Civilizations – the former Prime Minister of India, I. K. Gujral, as well as the social scientist and entrepreneur Jagdish Kapur, and Nicholas Papanicolaou, an American of Greek origin who had long been an advocate of the ecumenical movement – were an early indication of the plurality of voices we wanted to encourage; our very first conference in Delhi was attended by scholars, activists and politicians from many other countries.

Others who played a significant role in the early years were the Iranian Mohammad Khatami and the Lithuanian Valdas Adamkus, both of whom were former presidents of their countries. (My friendship with Adamkus, who fought against the Soviet Union before his family fled to the United States, and then spent the next fifty years on the other side of the cold war to myself, is a good example of the virtues of concentrating on what can be achieved by working together for a better future, rather than allowing oneself to become trapped by the battles and resentments of the past.) It has evolved now into an institution that is as cosmopolitan as the United Nations, with representatives from countries including India, China, Czech Republic, Poland, Cyprus, Austria and Greece.

After the attack on the Twin Towers in September 2001, our task suddenly felt more urgent. The atrocity itself and also the dangerous overreaction that followed were visceral examples of exactly what we wanted to avoid. They showed the extent to which empty rhetoric can be transformed into lethal action. The atrocity was not in itself an example of the clash of civilisations; it was an attack by a specific terrorist group, against a specific object, in a specific society. But the Western media, and many politicians, depicted these isolated events in far grander, more sweeping terms: as the embodiment of the profound antagonism that existed between two irreconcilable ways of life. Their arguments were so persuasive that they effectively became that oldest of clichés: a self-fulfilling prophecy. In this case, though, it was a cliché that has had disastrous consequences. The most tangible result of the 'War Against Terror' was a great flourishing of terrorism across the globe.

In the years since then, we have formed a close working relationship with the Alliance of Civilizations, a body created by the United Nations, which shares many of the same ambitions as the DOC. Like us, they recognise the benefits of offering people from different countries a way to communicate that is not mediated by the agendas of diplomats or media conglomerates.

We took another step forward in 2016 when we opened the Dialogue of Civilizations Research Institute in Berlin. It was, as much as anything, a recognition of the complexity of the issues facing us. Good sentiments and fine words have their place, but we wanted to ensure they were buttressed by cutting-edge research into the political, social and economic aspects of contemporary life. It has been designed as an independent body, supported by representatives from the worlds of business, politics and academia, that offers intellectual alternatives to some aspects of what one might term mainstream ideology. I would like to think that within the next few years the DOC Research Institute will be considered one of the ten or fifteen top think tanks in the world, joining the ranks of the centres of expertise whose work has a genuine influence on policy formation and academic debate. Our other central aim, one which governs every element of the DOC's activity, remains the same: to promote dialogue among people and societies, and to try and influence states and global powers, Russia included. It is a diffuse ambition, the success of which is nearly impossible to measure, but who could honestly say that it is not a worthwhile one?

We are not against the idea of development and economic growth, or people becoming richer, but we do not subscribe to the spiritually impoverished vision that reduces man to a consumer rather than a citizen – we want to foster programmes that place morality not materialism at the centre of human identity. Over four million babies died in 2016 – most could have been saved with the right kind of medication or care. Millions of people are starving in Africa every year. How can we not stop this when the world's GDP is worth over $75 trillion annually?

This is the message I have been promulgating for fifteen years. Not just at the Rhodes Forum, but across the world, at conferences, in articles. But, of course, our every step is attended by accusations that we are a front for a Putin-led propaganda campaign, while in Russia, by contrast, the very fact that we are not a state organisation and are not promoting the state's policies means that it is very difficult to secure coverage of our activities. There is not much one can do when some people continue to believe that the possession of a Russian passport means that one is inevitably an agent of the Kremlin. All I would ask is that they examine the work we have conducted already, or the statements we have issued. They will see nothing there that is designed to promote one set of values to the exclusion of all others – and why would there be, given that to do so would be a betrayal of everything the DOC was set up to achieve? When you see people attacking an organisation that has been created to promote openness and peace, then it shows the scale of the task before us. It would be funny if it were not also so dangerous.

CHAPTER NINE

THINGS FALL APART

The Holy Fire. No other miracle is known to occur with such regularity, taking place at the same time, in the same place, for eleven centuries. Each year, on the day preceding Orthodox Easter, in the Church of the Resurrection in Jerusalem, a blue light emanates from within Jesus Christ's tomb, eventually forming a column of flame. Moments later candles and lamps around the whole church are lit from this fire.

Thousands of pilgrims gather to witness and participate in this prodigious occurrence, and a handful will also convey the Holy Fire back to churches in their own countries. It is an event that is tightly embroidered into the fabric of the Orthodox Church, an institution that is in turn one of the threads from which Russian history and culture is woven. For over a millennium, the church was one of the primary methods for transmitting information about my nation's traditions and values from one generation to another. But during the Soviet era, it seemed that this thread might be broken for ever.

The Bolsheviks were not interested in accumulating money

or smart houses for themselves; they wanted to create a new, better world for the people of their country, and were willing to sacrifice everything to fight for the best future for the working class.

And yet the only instrument they had at hand was the destruction of much of our nation's history. In order to forcefully introduce a reluctant population to their cherished ideals of brotherhood and freedom, they tried to cut us adrift from a set of beliefs and values that had once run right through the heart of Russian life. They would create citizens who were not just convinced of the virtues of socialism, but who could not even consider the possibility of living under another kind of system.

Their year-zero approach meant that they had an antagonistic relationship with almost anything that occurred before 1917. In the new society they were building, the thousand-odd years of Russian culture and history that preceded the revolution had little use outside of an oversimplified kind of pedagogy: the tsars (with the honourable exceptions of Ekaterina and Peter the Great) were presented as murderers and fools who had existed only to advertise the benefits of socialism.

Lenin and his followers were avid for the complete transformation of society, and the comprehensiveness of their ambitions for intruding into the lives of its citizens was unprecedented. They were not content with simply seizing the means of production, or control of the government – the Communists wanted to mould a new kind of human, *Homo Sovieticus*.

This process began in Russia and over the next seventy years would be replicated across the whole of Eastern Europe, as well as much of Asia, Africa and Latin America. All political opposition was crushed and the public sphere was colonised by a totalitarian incarnation of socialism that crept into every corner of the people's lives. The Bolsheviks went to war against the pillars of civil society: the church, private enterprise and a free-thinking intelligentsia. Peasant traditions – the stories and memories passed on from one generation to another, which had always been a significant element in the transmission of cultural information in Russia – were another object of great suspicion. The press became a vehicle for propaganda, holidays simply an opportunity to conduct vast parades celebrating the regime's benevolence. The old ways of education were infiltrated, banned or simply left to rot, and in their place the state stepped in to ensure that it alone was responsible for forming the minds of future citizens. Textbooks were rewritten; teachers, priests and professors who were considered to be in possession of reactionary tendencies were replaced with pliable, ideologically correct substitutes; and all organisations that were not directly controlled by the Communist Party were proscribed.

Although the revolution created a range of opportunities for the poor and dispossessed that would have been unimaginable before 1917, it also introduced restrictions on the lives of many who had flourished under the tsars. With the gift for coining macabre neologisms that distinguished them, the Bolsheviks dismissed these so-called class enemies as 'former people'. A 'clean' autobiography became ever more important. For instance, life was made extremely difficult for Christians. Thousands of churches were destroyed, including the Cathedral of Christ the Saviour in Moscow (which was replaced with a swimming pool), and, very pointedly, no places of worship were built in the many new towns and cities that were being created across the country. Society as a whole was permeated with a very negative attitude towards religion: you would see it on television, hear it on the radio, read it in books – an atmosphere that seeped through your skin.

And while most Christians were not subject to outright persecution, if you professed your faith too publicly you would find your life pinched by a thousand tiny restrictions. The children of a priest could not join the Komsomol or the Communist Party, for instance, and church services were largely suppressed. A friend of mine, who is now a bishop, was not allowed during his military service to carry weapons because he was a believer. Instead, he was sent to a special construction regiment whose ranks were filled with the dregs of society. He was regularly beaten by the drunken men who were supposed to be his comrades, and when he was not the subject of their abuse he suffered under his unit's savage discipline. But he endured it.

It was only later that Soviet leaders came to understand that it is not possible to fight history. During the Great Patriotic War, many previously incarcerated clerics were released so that they could perform church services for people whose morale had been shot to pieces by the shocking and humiliating sequence of defeats suffered by the Red Army after the Nazi invasion. This was complemented by the introduction of military awards that explicitly referenced heroic figures from the country's past, such as Alexander Nevsky, as well as the reappropriation of the term 'Motherland'. Yet even with these manipulative compromises, most Russians were alienated from their past. For example, party leaders under Nikita Khrushchev sold off sacred land that had once belonged to the Russian Empire. They had no connection to it and thus felt little compunction at doing so. A huge site in the middle of Jerusalem, formerly the site of the Russian Religious Mission, was given up to the Israelis in return for a small amount of cash. Unable to pay in cash, the Israelis offered oranges instead. The freedoms that accompanied Khrushchev's reign were not extended to the church, which instead endured a renewed bout of repression at his hands.

By the time I was born, traces of the pre-revolutionary attitudes to faith and nationhood had survived, but they were only fragmentary and diffident. The ambiguous position Russia enjoyed within the Soviet Union meant that many Russians had a somewhat confused national identity. For years, the terms 'Russian' and 'Soviet' had been elided. And the vigorous repression of traditional identities meant that generations grew up with an unclear notion of what it really meant to be Russian – much of our heritage, with the exception of those elements that the Bolsheviks had coopted for their own purposes, had been suppressed or allowed to decay.

My mother had to arrange for me to be baptised in secret, an event that was hidden even from my father. As a Communist Party member, he could not be implicated in this conspiracy; if it had been discovered that he knew anything then he was at risk of punishment. I would not even say my mother was particularly religious, but I think she understood the importance of tradition. We would visit churches when I was young, and we would pray, but our engagement was as much about maintaining a connection with our country's customs and heritage as it was about religious observance.

But I did not, at least to begin with, understand the scale of our nation's loss, for I had been born into a happy generation. We were the children of the Khrushchev thaw, a period of openness and calm that was in stark contrast to the violence and cynicism of High Stalinism. The country had been in almost permanent turmoil since 1917, but the Civil War, the rural nightmare of collectivisation and the savage and uncertain years of the purges and five-year-plans were memories now. A nation ravaged by one of the most brutal and destructive conflicts in history – that between 1941 and 1945 had lost more than 26 million citizens – had been able to send a man into space just sixteen years later.

Like everyone around me, I grew up convinced that socialism was inevitable and that, within my lifetime, it would reign throughout the world, bringing with it peace, equality and a better standard of living for everyone. There was a true sense of community and cohesion and we did not worry about the future. Like my peers, I felt, more than anything, free. We were encouraged to follow our dreams, and the country in which we lived provided us with the tools to achieve them.

From an early age, we were all participants in a comprehensive programme designed to introduce the entire population to the socialist principles that underpinned our society. At twelve, we joined the Pioneers and then, when we were into our teens, the Komsomol. We were taught how to be good citizens: to make friends, to help each other, to take special care to help the elderly, to respect our parents, to love our country, to try and contribute to the wellbeing of the communities in which we lived.

We were brought up on the examples of the heroes of the Patriotic War of 1812 and the Great Patriotic War of 1941–45, and learned about the achievements of socialists across the world. We were encouraged to feel proud of our education system, of our cosmonauts' brave journeys into outer space, and also of the advances that had been made by our fellow progressives. When Fidel Castro visited the USSR in 1963, he was mobbed in the street by children who had escaped from their schools just so they could greet this hero; they were joined by their parents and friends – so many people that the police struggled to control the excitement.

Once we left school and started to work, we would discover that every factory, every shop, had some kind of representative from the regime's local apparatus. Our lives, whether we always were conscious of it or not, were permeated by the values of socialism, and by the time we reached adulthood, the vast majority of us shared the same ideals, and were all committed to achieving the same targets.

Socialism was a system that had given us all a great deal and which we regarded as superior to the selfish, bloated and unequal capitalist regimes we learned about in our textbooks, even if it was not without its own faults. When you consider where my forebears had come from, then perhaps this confidence does not seem so misplaced. My father, who eventually would go on to be a highly respected pilot in the Soviet Frontier Guards – was born into a family of poor peasants in central Russia. It seemed to them like a miracle when he graduated from the military academy in Moscow. Sputnik was launched in 1957, when I was nine, but the most significant event for his parents that year was that they finally got electricity in their home – it is hard not to think of Lenin's famous saying: 'Communism is Soviet power plus the electrification of the entire country'. There was no golden age for my forebears to look back on to compare – generations had led lives scarred by poverty and exclusion.

I remember that a little later, when I was still a young boy, their household was afflicted by a tragedy: their cow passed away. It seems inconceivable now, but they depended on that animal; indeed, they were far from alone in relying on such a fragile thread for their survival. My father was forced to give his family his entire officer's salary, together with loans from friends – 4,000 roubles, if I remember correctly; an enormous sum at the time – because he understood that they would die without it. At exactly the same time as large swathes of Russia were under-going enormous urbanisation and industrialisation, and millions of previously impoverished citizens were offered new hope and dignity, they were part of a shadow population, left behind and forgotten by the modern world.

Though I was born only twenty-nine years after my father, the advantages I enjoyed compared to him meant that we might as well have been raised in different centuries. Those living in the first years of communism suffered terribly; they sacrificed their comfort so that we might enjoy a different kind of life. Despite the terrible losses suffered in the Great Patriotic War, by 1948 our nation had made many decades' worth of progress in just one generation. Unlike our parents, my friends and I did not grow up stalked by hunger or frustrated by ignorance. We felt safe, well fed and secure in the knowledge that we would be receiving one of the best educations available anywhere in the world. Under the tsars, only a minority of the population had been able to read, whereas the Bolsheviks introduced compulsory universal education and built thousands of schools – I grew up in an almost completely literate society, where books were cheap and writers valued. Even in the 1930s, a time when many capitalist nations were struggling with the effects of a crippling global depression, there was close to full employment in the Soviet Union, and the same remained true when I came of age. By the time I was a teenager, it felt as if the only question that hung over us was: what would you like to be when you are older? A doctor? An engineer? A scientist?

It helped that few of us were afraid of sacrifice. We were aware of the concept of political necessity – that in order to achieve great aims, sometimes small things must be sacrificed along the way. We were prepared to put up with the occasional shortage, the incursions by the state into our private lives, the crumbling apartment blocks that stank of beer and stale smoke, because we were patriots confident that whatever we endured would be for the greater good and that the final triumph of socialism was in sight.

Later, I would come to learn about the Soviet Union's dissidents, or 'other-thinkers' as they referred to themselves, whose relationship with the state and its ideology diverged sharply from the position I had taken, and who wanted their lives to unfurl in different ways to the rest of the population (although it is worth mentioning that, more often than not, their criticisms were of the way in which the USSR had veered away from the true path set out by Lenin all those years ago; it was rare that any argued for imitating the capitalistic systems of the West, which would not have occurred to people who knew nothing but a Communist regime). I knew of people who had been sent to camps, but at the time it remained a peripheral kind of knowledge, glimpsed as it were out of the corners of my eyes; it did not trespass on my loyalty.

I never had any problems with the system myself – why would I, when it had given me and my family everything? I felt free; I did not need to pretend to be something I was not, or articulate opinions I did not share. It is too easy – too convenient – to say that in the Soviet Union we were automatons who ate, dressed, danced or thought in exactly the same way. Even within the KGB, where you might imagine people would be dogmatic ideologists determined to control your every move, there was space for pragmatic, humane behaviour. Early on in my career, my sister became engaged to an unsavoury character who, by any measure (political or moral), was profoundly unsuitable. Because I knew that my sister was desperate to start a family, I offered to resign from my post: I could not stand in the way of her happiness, but nor did I wish to risk compromising my work or that of my colleagues in any way. Rather than accepting, as I had expected, my director simply told me that since it was a personal issue, it did not concern him or the agency. And that, as far as he was concerned, was that.

This freedom, this generally positive attitude towards the system, was not incompatible with being aware of some of its faults. In the early 1970s, after having graduated from the Leningrad Mechanical Institute, I was a researcher at the State Institute of Applied Chemistry in Leningrad. I had been asked to speak at a big conference attended by all the local party and Komsomol bosses. The idea was that I would deliver a report eulogising the inevitable fulfilment of the country's latest economic plan – which, it had just been announced, would be completed in just four years, rather than the initially proclaimed five – and condemning Aleksandr Solzhenitsyn's novel, *One Day in the Life of Ivan Denisovich*.

It was fashionable then to compare the respective productivity of the USSR and the USA. Because it appeared from the calculations we were privy to that our country's output per capita was about half of that achieved in America, the idea was that the gap would be made up by keeping the machinery on in factories right through the night, and scheduling three different working shifts per day. The other area in which it was felt that significant improvements could be made was in the countryside – would it not be better, the theory ran, if farms were organised to run more like factories?

I was not at all confident that simply having the machinery running almost permanently would lead to an increase in productivity – in fact, I feared the opposite. For one thing, I remember my mother telling me the reason why she had left her job as an accountant at a factory in Leningrad. At that time, the targets set by the Gosplan, the central planning agency, related not only to what you were expected to produce (it did not matter if your goods were shoddy, or that there was no demand from them, as long as you hit your goals everything was fine), but also how much material you were expected to use in order to do so. And the logic of this system dictated that if you built a house, and an inspector noticed that you had not employed your full allotted quantity of concrete to do so, you were liable to be punished.

This led to ludicrous activity: men deliberately wasting precious building materials, workers frantically trying to dispose of a lump of half-drying concrete in a field before anybody noticed. And in those cases where a breach of the rules was detected, it was invariably the accountant who was sent to jail. My mother did not believe she should be held responsible for the infractions of others. So I did not need to be told that a decision made in an office in Moscow did not always translate into effective action.

As strong as the party's centralising impulse and calls for obedience were, they were never sufficient to overmaster the incompetence and dishonesty of some of its citizens. Especially since many of its officials deliberately supplied their superiors with misinformation, so that those charged with planning the country's future were rarely if ever furnished with the facts they needed to build up a picture of the economic landscape. Official schemes always had to coexist with the illicit and disordered. And though I was no expert on agriculture, I knew enough to be aware that it was not like urban industrial processes, where the same work could be completed throughout the year. In the rural villages, life was still necessarily dictated by the changing seasons; no matter how sincere the party's ambition to increase the yield was, it could not stop summer churning relentlessly into autumn and then winter.

So instead of the praise for our increased productivity that I might have been expected to deliver, I said, 'Listen, in the Soviet Union we have a planned economy, but I cannot understand how we can fulfil the plan, not in five years, but in four years. What kind of planning do we have?'

'As for Solzhenitsyn,' I continued, 'there is little I can say for I have not read the book in question. If what I have heard about the substance of the book is right, then, yes, I disagree with that. Yet I cannot condemn something that I have not seen with my own eyes.'

Nothing that came out of my mouth that day was in any way conventional. It was the kind of thing you might expect to hear from dissidents, but later on the most senior party representative in the room praised me. Indeed, when he returned to the local headquarters, he called his subordinates together to tell them that, even if they might not agree with the awkward direction my thoughts were heading in, it was important to listen to criticisms made by young men like me. Not long afterwards, I was elected head of the Institute's Komsomol organisation. There may have been a script, but there was also far more room for improvisation than many people who grew up in the West would imagine. The state was a sprawling, multifarious beast that always struggled to accommodate demands made by numerous different interest groups. Totalitarianism was certainly at the heart of the regime's ambitions, but in a country as large, complex and unruly as the Soviet Union, it was never possible to achieve complete, unmediated control.

The secret service gave me a panoramic, privileged view of Soviet society and I encountered everyone from academicians, the directors of factories and scientific institutes and artists and musicians, right through to prostitutes, the homeless and homosexuals. I travelled in Europe and was trusted with access to books, documents and ideas that were out of bounds to ordinary people, and I found out other, stranger, things too. How, for instance, the bosses of criminal societies and the top party leaders played cards and billiards together in the same closed clubs; that the party was honeycombed by careerists attracted by the prospects offered by the organisation that had the monopoly on power; or that, in order to meet their quotas, managers routinely provided their superiors with false reports.

But whatever else might be said about the Soviet Union, and however much damage had been wrought by the state's jealously maintained position as the sole source of education, I believe that this much is true: socialism was a story that gave meaning to all of our lives. Even by the '80s, when our grey cities were barely lit at night and it was almost impossible to get hold of coffee, even once we knew about the massacre at Novocherkassk, and the dead boys being brought back from Afghanistan in sealed zinc coffins, it told us where we were going, and why we were heading in that direction. It made us proud of our country and its achievements – whether that was universal education or the triumph in the Great Patriotic War. If I might borrow a phrase from an unexpected quarter, socialism was our own shining city on a hill.

I remember reading an account once about an interesting experiment. A dog was put in a room with two plates of food, one of which was attached to an electrical current. When the dog tried to eat from the electrified plate, it received a shock. After a couple of unpleasant encounters, it learned to leave that plate alone and focused its efforts on the safe plate on the other side of the room. But the scientists then wired up both plates. Once the dog discovered that he would be subjected to a nasty shock no matter which dish he chose to eat from, he simply laid down and went to sleep. The researchers concluded that the dog was so stunned and bewildered by the cruel circumstance he had found himself in that, unable to understand what was going on, he gave up and entered into a kind of hibernation.

After the dissolution of the Soviet Union, the population was introduced to a similar kind of mental stress. People were exposed to challenges they had never been confronted with before, but nobody explained to them why they were being forced to suffer like this. We were all enthused by the freedoms offered by the democratic system that had been brought in with such fanfare, and yet we no longer knew what it meant to be Russian. The collapse of the Communist system was not just a political or administrative event; it was a moral catastrophe that robbed an entire society of the norms and ethics that had guided its citizens' lives for over seven decades, and replaced them with a single imperative: if an act is not expressly forbidden by law, then anything goes.

A healthy, confident culture can absorb ideas from other countries, taking what works in its particular context, and rejecting what does not fit. But in Russia during the '90s, with the state having abdicated its role as provider of ideology and cohesion, we imported whole systems of thought and belief from the West without any sense of how they might fit with our own. They did not complement what we had already; instead, they began to destroy it. Society became atomised and many people began to privilege self-interest and profit above the communal values with which we had all been raised. (I do not trust anyone who claims they can happily exist alone, without the comforting, sustaining exchanges that come from living alongside others. It is not natural for a human being.) We soon discovered, to our cost, that though it is easy to create consumers – you could build branches of McDonald's, sell Levi's jeans, import Mercedes cars, and the whole process needed only a few nudges from the state before it was up and running – it is far more difficult to create a healthy, functioning democratic culture overnight. We had none of the institutions of civil society, and the old traditions that for centuries had been the connective tissue that bound the country together had been allowed to wither away. When the country was hit by a succession of crises that exposed its new weakness, society crumbled.

We needed to be given a narrative that explained who we were and where we were going, and why that was a good thing, but with communism defeated, and the old methods of transmitting cultural information long-destroyed, there was now a huge vacuum where ideas and identity should have been. There was not a single political institution that was dedicated to the health of the society. It was not enough to be able go out and buy a new car or watch – especially since only a limited proportion of the population could afford these panaceas. These items were, we would learn, little more than a sticking plaster.

Clerical organisations were the only bodies left with authority, the only bodies trying to heal the grievous wounds that had been inflicted on the Russian population. And perhaps it was not surprising that people responded as warmly to them as they did. We were, after all, a society suffused with belief (ever since the 1920s, there had been an understanding that many traditionally Christian values had been present in Communist ideology, so even though the faith itself was afforded no space, many of its tenets were already sewn into our souls), it was just that now there was nowhere we could turn to channel this emotion. A 'superstition' that the Bolsheviks had assumed would eventually crumble into dust had instead proved surprisingly durable. And what was true of the Orthodox Church in Russia was true also of Islam in the Caucuses, and of Judaism, which in the years since 1991 has enjoyed an astonishing, almost unparalleled renewal.[21]

For those people who did not know where their lives were heading, or to whom they could turn, the church or mosque or synagogue became a place they could visit and find somebody who at least tried to listen to their concerns and reassure them. If they were hungry, they might even find a meal. These places of worship became a source of hope to men and women who had lost everything, and while there were few attempts at proselytisation, I think many rediscovered the religion that had lain dormant within them for most of their lives.

It was out of respect for the great service they provided that I began to communicate with members of the priesthood and also to start contributing money from my own pocket. In the years since my clandestine baptism, my relationship with Christianity had evolved, albeit slowly. Once I became an officer and had embarked on my adult, professional life, I came to believe that although our understanding of the physical world was expanding

---

21 Much Western coverage of Russia has tended to focus on the somewhat misleading contention that Orthodox Christianity has become a kind of adjunct of the state, but this is an unfortunately one-eyed view of the religious landscape in Russia. While 80 per cent of the population would self-identify as Christian, church attendance rarely struggles above 4 per cent. Compare this to the Eid celebrations, in which 250,000 Muslims spill into the streets of Moscow. Russia contains Europe's biggest mosque and 10 per cent of its population is Muslim. All this should be kept in mind by anyone tempted to make generalisations about the country.

more quickly than at any previous time in human history, we still knew little or nothing about metaphysical life. Perhaps, I concluded, there was something else we could not understand, that remained forever out of our grasp.

I only really came to the church relatively late in life, in 2003, at the age of fifty-four. It was in that year that, for the first time, along with a group of others, we brought the Holy Fire from Jerusalem to Moscow, in time for the Easter service at the Christ the Saviour cathedral – the resumption of a ritual abandoned under communism, and one we have reprised every year since. I believed that anything that could bring people together, which could provide support and inspiration to the people left disillusioned by the collapse of the USSR, could only be positive.

To begin with, I considered the initiative more from that perspective and did not consider myself religious at all; I did not even cross myself as I entered the church, since I believed it would be an act of hypocrisy. It took three years for me to be able to come to some kind of accommodation within my soul, so I could reconcile myself to the truth of what I was actually engaged in.

And even today, I would hesitate before proclaiming that I should be called devout. (I know I am not a perfect man, far from it, but I know too that I have never betrayed anybody, nor have I ever used my position to harm somebody as a means of advancing my own selfish interests.) To deserve that description, there are many rules that must be followed, many pieties observed – and the life I have led, and the life I lead now, discount me from this. I have little time and I am constantly travelling, but my belief runs deep.

Homo sapiens emerged on the savannahs of Africa around a hundred thousand years ago. We evolved family and community structures as ways of ensuring survival in an often hostile, unforgiving environment. Domestic life, caring for the future of your children, working for the common wealth of the people you live alongside, fair treatment of other members of society – all these are rooted in the prehistory of mankind, hardwired into our consciousness. As societies developed, these qualities were joined by other things worth celebrating: people learned about rights and responsibilities and, through freedom of speech and democracy, discovered new ways of being free.

It is only in the past thirty years, as post-modernity's moral relativity has been absorbed into the bloodstreams of societies across the world, that these values, which we had become accustomed to regarding as inherent in mankind, have become increasingly threatened. Other assaults have come from the mass media – which, rather than reflecting society, increasingly seems determined to be the force that shapes it – and, perhaps most insidiously, the technological innovations that are altering the world around us at an almost incomputable rate. How can we hold on to our humanity when the rate of development in, inter alia, information technology, communication technology, biotechnology and artificial intelligence is outstripping our ability to even comprehend it, let alone control it?

Russia has still not managed to evolve a coherent set of morals and ethics that can fill the void left by the collapse of communism, or insulate it from the dangers of the twenty-first century. This nation of 200 nations, of more than 140 million souls, needs a guiding philosophy to ensure that its centre can hold. We need a story that we can tell about ourselves that will help explain who we are, and why it is worth our while to persist even when storm clouds begin to gather. Otherwise, as we know from grim experience, things fall apart.

I do not believe that a person can be forced to be good (bad, yes, but that is a different matter). Values are not something that can be imposed from above; they cannot be the result of legislation – those of us who have experienced communism, or its legacy, at first hand know in our bones the truth of this – or forcing people to go to church every Sunday. (In the course of the twentieth century, we saw how every project designed to create a new human being failed catastrophically, with unbearable costs. In the West, I can see ever greater attempts to make morality and ethics a question of legal fiat rather than consensus – who knows how the *Homo Europeanus* experiment will end?) The creation, or recovery, of a value-based society must instead be a consensual enterprise informed by the work of thinkers and theologians, and, perhaps most significantly, a deep if critical engagement with tradition and history: no new story, no new body of ethics, can ever proceed from a policy of oblivion.

In Russian, the word for education, *vospitanie*, means more than simply the classes a child takes at school; it is also about introducing them to the best of their traditions and culture. *Vospitanie* involves developing one's character and values, not just acquiring academic qualifications. This is why the degradation of education, which is in many ways also the degradation of culture, has been one of the great tragedies of the post-Soviet era. If you want to rebuild a society's moral core, then you need an understanding of what was lost in the first place. Instead, schools and universities that once were the envy of the world have been left to languish and decay as state spending on education was halved between 1990 and 1995, becoming symbols of the country's lack of faith in its future.

For over seventy years, the CPSU monopolised almost every element of the people's cultural and social formation, cutting ties with folk traditions and the beneficial effects of civil society and swarming into every corner of people's lives, and it left a vacuum once the Soviet Union collapsed. If, since 1991, schools have been unable to transmit a sense of *vospitanie* to their pupils (though of course the burden should not fall on their shoulders alone), it is more important than ever that other institutions step up and provide it.

Once such institution is, of course, the family, which has been a constant source of refuge and resilience for Russians through-out history, and remains one of the most important bulwarks against the alienation and loss that threatens us all. Few better vehicles for the transmission of culture and values have ever been invented, and the warmth and support provided by families is ever more important in an increasingly atomised, morally con-fused world.

I am a secularist who believes in the separation of church and state, but there is no doubt that the Russian Orthodox Church is another institution that can play a role in this process. It has always been central to the history of our nation, as well as in the development of our civilisation, and amid the humiliation and misery of those dreadful years after the end of the Soviet Union, the Orthodox faith provided succour and support to many thou-sands of my fellow Russians – a service to the nation of almost incalculable value. Alongside this, its endeavours have helped to preserve the best and most important of Russia's traditions.

Charities are another potential pillar of a values-based society. I personally am closely involved with The Foundation of Andrew The First-Called. I have been a member of the Foundation since 1998, and a number of years ago I became chairman of its board.

Its creation was inspired by the work of St Andrew, known to Russian Orthodox believers as Andrew The First-Called. It was Andrew who first preached the Gospel in Russia and what is now known as Ukraine, and he remains an important figure, especially among members of the Russian Navy, for whom he acts as a patron saint. The foundation was established with the idea that through education, publications and public activity, it would be able to celebrate the great historical achievements of Russia and its population, and to communicate our nation's heritage and values to younger generations. We want to promote responsibility to other people and to the environment in which we live, as well as the idea that service to our country should be an important element of every citizen's mentality.

We are involved in and support religious and social events. Alongside more numinous activities such as public processions, pilgrimages (most famously from Vladivostok to Moscow) and the restoration of churches, monasteries and nunneries across Russia, there have also been unambiguously secular events such as historical conferences, or our attempts to restore a monument to the Russians who died in the Crimea between 1920–21, the result of a forced evacuation during our Civil War.

What connects these two strands is a single vision: we want to preserve our historical heritage and values and strengthen the

Russian people's connection to them. We know that the past century has, for many Russians, been full of pain, struggle and suffering. Wounds opened a century ago have still not been closed. This is why we have been at the forefront of attempts to heal them. With this in mind, we have worked hard to try and effect a reconciliation between the various fragments of the Russian Orthodox Church,[22] which looked to have split irrevocably in those years when our nation was divided by blood and anger. By facilitating the return of some of our faith's most holy relics to Russia and encouraging dialogue between each confession's leading figures, we aim to bring people from both sides closer to each other, joined by the understanding that whatever differences we may all have had in the past, we have only one homeland, and that it is our responsibility to restore and cherish it. It is a reconciliation that will, we hope, affect the lives of those living within our borders, but also the ten-million-strong Russian diaspora – those people and their descendants who have been scattered across the globe by the cruel winds that have blown through our recent history.

We have helped with the preservation of the Russian cemetery in Paris and, just as significantly, the archives contained within the city. These, which are probably the largest Russian archives outside of the Princeton Library, were on the brink of being destroyed because there was nowhere to store them. We were able, together with the émigré community there, to fundraise and create a programme that would ensure its preservation.

---

22 Notably, the Moscow Patriarchate and the Russian Orthodox Church Abroad, which was set up in New York in the 1920s by émigrés who refused to recognise the former's authority once it had, as they saw it, fallen under the control of the Bolsheviks.

A bright future is not possible without an understanding of the past, for without a strong sense of the connection between past and present and without knowing about all the many thousands of ways in which what has gone before informs what we are living through now, we run the risk of becoming, in a sense, orphans.

It was with this spirit in mind that in 2017 we launched a project called 'Russia 1917. Images of the Future'. Users of social networks were presented with the programmes offered by the various political groupings that were vying for power in Russia in that transformational year.

What surprised all of us was that the youngest participants voted almost overwhelmingly in favour of the policies and vision offered by the Bolsheviks. But perhaps we should not have been taken so off-guard. Their generation wants a new project: they want to have the chance to play an active role in shaping an alternative future for the world, one that allows individual nations to become more than just pallid, dependent imitations of the United States; they recognise that GDP growth is an arid, impoverished rubric for a nation's health – it says little about a population's happiness, or about their hopes and fears for the future; and they want to be part of a country that *means* something.

This was an ideal that was once represented by the Bolsheviks. The Soviet Union, for all its manifold faults, was a competitor to the West. Its existence alone was a challenge to the world of capitalism and profit; it offered the promise of a different, fairer, way of arranging a nation's business. So while perhaps there was something unanticipated about their support for the Bolsheviks, their desire for a change seems to be of a piece with much of what I see happening around me as I write this.

There was a time when many of the things we talked about at the Foundation and also at the Dialogue of Civilizations were regarded as illusions, almost insulting to professional economics. But I think things are changing. Terms like 'neo-liberal orthodoxy', which were almost outlawed years ago, are now a matter of common currency. I spoke with the head of a New York-based economic think tank recently. I told him that I was struck by the fact that in a recent speech he had stated that we were in the depths of a crisis. In his response to me, he began his analysis of the situation with a discussion of values, something that has not hitherto been acknowledged to have any connection with the economic models that have governed our world for the past twenty years. I asked him: if we are talking about a crisis in the world today, should we really be saying that we are talking about a crisis in humanity? Without pausing for a second, he said yes. It was a conversation that could not have taken place even five years ago – that it was possible shows both how serious the issues we're facing are, but also that perhaps a new kind of consensus is emerging that might help us solve them.

This is becoming the new mainstream discussion. Whatever you think about the extraordinary shocks in 2016 that have left much of the conventional wisdom about the world and the way it works in tatters, one thing is clear: people are tired of the political paradigm that has reigned for so long. They want to dismantle the existing system and replace it with something that works for them, not rich corporations or entitled elites. I believe that, increasingly, there is a demand not only for different answers, but for different questions entirely. If we are going to have a conversation about inequality, or the way in which tension and violence might mount in a particular country, then we need to address the anthropological basis, to start thinking about values and how they have to be returned to the centre of our social and political lives: simply growing a country's GDP by a couple of percentage points is no longer an adequate response. People are, finally, looking for something more.

EPILOGUE

The past is always with us. It is never over; it will never lose its power. No action or event ever really disappears, even if sometimes it may seem as though it has receded from view.

In 1991 I thought that the cold war had died along with the Soviet Union. I wondered if everything we had lost would, in part, be compensated by all that we would gain in a new era – one in which the tensions and suspicion that had characterised the decades since 1945 would ebb away. It did not. Perhaps for a while it went into something like hibernation, but now it is becoming clear that it never really left.

Perhaps to you it may seem as if Donald Trump has radically altered the direction of the United States' foreign policy; that under Putin's influence (as some people argue) the President has relaxed his country's position towards Russia. But the way I see it, although he has largely eschewed the kind of rhetoric Hillary Clinton would probably have employed had she won, in real terms this makes little difference. Consider, for instance, the decision by Congress earlier this year to impose an extended range of sanctions and to use its influence in Western Europe to ensure that the force of the sanctions is felt. Or the US's newly published National Security Strategy, which casts Russia (along with China) as a 'revisionist power' that seeks to 'challenge American power, influence and interests', while 'attempting to erode American security and prosperity'.

The skeletons of the cold war are up and walking about once more. And with every passing day they become stronger. Some politicians in both Russia and the West have avoided using the term, and yet I cannot see that they will be able to do so for much longer. It is high time to start calling it what it is.

Of course there is no longer the same wide ideological gap; one can find few places in the world now where the markets do not reign (although places like China, India and Russia have all modified the model to suit their own particular circumstances). And yet while classic capitalism is no longer ranged against pure socialism, and loyalties across the world have been realigned (the Warsaw Pact now seems as much of an anachronism as the Hanseatic League or the Triple Entente[23]), it seems that once more the West is at odds with Russia.

After 1991, we never felt as if we were welcomed into the

---

23 This may read like a crude characterisation, but I would argue that a new divide has split the world. On one side there are all the nations in the West who adhere to a neo-liberal model of politics and economics, and believe that the rest of the world should be encouraged to adopt the same values. For them, there is only one route to prosperity and civilisation. I see this as a form of chauvinism that is not only insensitive, but which, it is becoming increasingly clear, has failed on its own terms. There is no attempt to understand local conditions or listen to local terms, which means that their interventions invariably come to resemble the damage caused by a bull in a china shop.

The other side bears little resemblance to the relatively cohesive socialist bloc of the twentieth century's second half. In comparison to the united Western system, it is dispersed and disparate. There is little that China, or the Arab nations, or even the central European countries that have joined the EU but have remained on its periphery, have in common, except that they have chosen to push back against attempts to force their culture and economies into a shape that pleases the politicians of the developed world.

international community as an equal partner; it seemed as if there was an expectation that we should behave like a suppliant. And yet those days now seem like a brief golden age of cooperation and hope, when something better seemed possible. That hope has been replaced by suspicion and the old temptation to demonise Russia has returned.

One could perhaps argue that to a large extent, the security, political and military establishments of Russia and the West alike are still populated by people who came of age when the cold war was at its height, and have never managed (or wanted) to rid themselves of the assumptions and prejudices that were instilled in them more than three decades ago. This situation has been exacerbated by the pressure placed by US-led Western institutions on Russia in the years following 1991 to adhere to an economic and political model that was inimical to its traditions and historical experience. Russia was never fully integrated into the new global order that emerged after the collapse of the Soviet Union; instead we have seen the kind of cultural friction predicted in Samuel P. Huntington's theories about the clash of civilisations.

It feels to me now as if all the black spots on the face of human existence are laid at Russia's door. I can understand why. There is after all something seductive about the idea that one nation alone is responsible for the world's problems. It allows people to forget for a moment how phenomenally complex a planet we live on and to convince themselves that if only this one nation could be brought to heel, its leader muzzled, then all would be well. It also enables them to overlook how comparatively weakened Russia really is. Sometimes I wish we really were the omnipresent, omnipotent force we are sometimes painted as being!

But this situation also means that people are afraid. A climate has emerged which means that they do not feel comfortable any more making the connections that are so sorely needed if we are to diffuse the tensions that are growing around us all the time. In 2017, we invited three prominent German writers to attend an event at the Dialogue of Civilizations in Berlin, a contemporary cultural interaction and exchange between Europe and the East under the title 'European Comedy'. Initially they were all eager to come, but when news of their potential participation became known, a couple were summoned to the institutions they worked for and were warned against involving themselves with a 'Kremlin propaganda organisation'. To attend, it was suggested, would prejudice their career prospects. It is an unpleasant paradox: without dialogue, the situation we are in will become ever more severe; and yet any attempts by people from the West to forge meaningful links with their Russian counterparts are treated with suspicion. Even in the US, Congressmen are afraid of talking with the Russian ambassador in case they find themselves embroiled in accusations of collusion and conspiracy.

I hate the idea that we have allowed ourselves to become so frozen by the new chill in relations between Russia and the West. Our ability to think for ourselves is under threat. It sometimes feels to me as if there are people on both sides of the divide trying to get into our brains in order to reshuffle the ideas and emotions they find there – manipulating information and filling us with propaganda in order to try and turn us into zombies who will do whatever we are ordered.

And we should never underestimate how profound an impact the messages that children are absorbing now will have on their outlook on the future. I do not want them to internalise the propaganda and the lies that have once again become common currency. If Russian children see only criticism of the West in their parents' newspapers, if English children only hear how evil Russians are when they turn on the television, it will entrench mentalities that will take years to overcome. There is no word spoken today that will not stay lodged inside the souls of those who will lead the world of tomorrow.

There is, in my opinion, a substantial discrepancy between the beliefs of the vast majority of most countries' populations, and those espoused by the cultural and political elites who govern them. Much of the information we have access to is controlled by a small number of people – the politicians, businessmen and newspaper editors who all frequent the same clubs, who all eat at the same restaurants – and so it tends to reflect a narrow perspective: it is rare that in either Russia or the West you will see any positive reflections on the other camp. The tone on both sides is overwhelmingly negative. And yet if you talk to men and women in the streets of the West, or of Russia, then the opinions they hold of each other's nations diverge greatly from those articulated by the people who claim to speak in their name. This, though, is of little use if they are consistently presented with a narrative of hostility and otherness.

To me, to be able to think, to feel compassion for another, is the essential element in what it is to be human. If your interests do not extend beyond filling your belly or satisfying your lust, then you may as well be a robot or an animal – and yet I fear that our capacity to empathise is being degraded.

If I met a younger incarnation of myself in the street tomorrow

I would urge him to remember always that other people inhabit very different perspectives. People's refusal to take this into account, to ignore the fact that others possess an outlook quite different to theirs, is the source of much of the discontent and friction in the world today, and prejudices our chances of emerging unscathed from the tensions that are enveloping us.

One salient example might be the consequences of NATO's expansion in Eastern Europe. In the West this is seen as an important element in establishing collective security, but in Russia it feels like a threat.

You need to remember that in Russia we have a different relationship with history: I think perhaps we have longer memories, so we are more easily affected when current events come to resemble the past. Though our nation has been turned upside down more than once in the past century, though the Bolsheviks implemented a systematic assault on its culture and traditions, still the connection we have with the experiences of previous generations is far stronger. The West has experienced successive waves of societal and political change, with each development replacing much of what had gone before – the cord is broken. (At times this might be the result of inattention, though at others – as in the case of the Japanese government's proposal to shut humanities departments in favour of 'more practical' subjects – it can be caused by a wilful impulse.)

So in England, for instance, I get the feeling that the Great Patriotic War is considered, when it is considered at all, as a long-distant triumph, like the Queen's Jubilee or the 1966 World Cup. These events have not been forgotten, but the passage of time has rubbed them smooth. They regard them as one might a fondly remembered film. By contrast, in Russia we are still haunted by the atrocities that followed the Nazi invasion in 1941. Our territory was ravaged, towns were burnt, immeasurable cruelty meted out to those unfortunate enough to fall into German hands. The memory of these crimes still flows in our veins – it cannot be reduced to an exercise in nostalgia – so perhaps it is not so strange that we are alarmed when we see foreign tanks and soldiers ranged along our borders. (Fears that have been stoked again by the recent publication of classified documents, which reveal how little the US Secretary of State James Baker's famous 'not one inch eastward' assurance about NATO expansion, which he made in a meeting with Mikhail Gorbachev in February 1990, was really worth.)

I do not mention this because I wish to suggest one side is worse than another – I am sure that an American could point to instances where Russia's actions have touched deep-rooted historical anxieties – but simply to illustrate the consequences of mutual incomprehension and the failure of empathy.[24]

In 1930, John Maynard Keynes predicted in his essay 'Economic Possibilities for Our Grandchildren' that, in the future, living standards in what he called progressive countries would advance to the stage where most people would have to work no more than fifteen hours a week. He believed that the population's material

---

24 You could argue that Russia's adverse geography has also had its own role in shaping the Russian mentality, far more so than in other countries. The harsh conditions, the sheer remoteness of so many communities, implanted a sense of solidarity in the Russian soul. It is the distinguishing element in our psychological make-up. Without this emphasis on the welfare of the man next door to you, without this acknowledgement of the extent to which we depend on others, and thus have corresponding responsibility for them ourselves, people would simply not have survived.

desires would be met so easily that the desire to earn more money would be regarded almost as a pathological illness. Freed from the battle for survival, they would be able to devote much of their time to pleasure and self-development. He was right in some respects – we live in what people in the '30s would have regarded as almost unimaginable luxury – and mistaken in many others.

When I returned to St Petersburg in 1991 we had very little, but we were happy. Now when I am in St Petersburg and Moscow I find myself surrounded by people who can have what they want, whenever they want it. You can find anything you want in the shops, enjoy food at some of the best restaurants in the world, stare at expensive cars and glinting skyscrapers, and yet despite these signs of conspicuous wealth, I do not believe that people are more content. Perhaps less so.

I remember how in those first years after the collapse of the Soviet Union my family and I were sustained by a belief in the future. Today has not been good, we would say, but tomorrow will be better. I thought then that people would be happier as soon as they were richer. It seems that, like Keynes, I was wrong.

The world has changed in so many ways, but I am not sure that I have changed with it, at least not deep inside, where one's true essence lies. Sometimes it seems to me that I have been like the still centre of a storm – while everything else has been ripped up and thrown to every corner of the wind, here I am, steady, much the same as I ever was. Occasionally I wonder what the young intelligence officer who travelled with his family to New York in 1985 to defend socialism would make of the man I have become; I hope he would see that I have held on to many of the same values that he cherished, that I still believe in solidarity and respect, that my love for my family and country are as strong as they were then.

Of course, the passing of the years has taken its toll on my body and I am increasingly conscious that the time left to me is limited. I know that I may not be able to achieve all the things I want to, and as a result I find myself gripped by an urgency that I never knew before.

I started writing this book in July 2016 in what already felt like very different circumstances. It was not designed as an exculpatory exercise; I do not need to be told that I am no saint. My intention then was only to show a different perspective to Western readers, one that I hoped would be frank and insightful.

But now as I sit here in December 2017 I am as alarmed as I ever was during the peak of the cold war. Spitak, Chernobyl, 9/11, all these events taught me how fragile life is, how vulnerable we all are – and that the same blood runs through all of our veins. The way that the Americans responded with such compassion to the earthquake in Armenia, a disaster that had befallen people in a distant nation that was supposed to be their enemy was a pivotal moment for me; it helped me understand that it was possible to transcend ideology and propaganda. I worry that our capacity to do this again is diminishing with every day that goes by. I still want to help people from the West understand my country and the reasons it views the world in the way it does, though I fear that perhaps this is no longer sufficient – something more is needed.

Had you asked me three years ago if I felt optimistic about the future then I would have replied yes without a second's pause. Now, things are different. I have to remind myself that despondency is one of the venial sins, so if you consider yourself a Christian, then you can never abandon hope, even if it seems as though the conditions for maintaining optimism are withering.

But we cannot sit idle waiting for a Messiah to come along and do our work for us. It is our responsibility, as citizens, to realise the power we possess. All human beings are able to produce something positive, to contribute to the health of civil society, both domestically and internationally. I will continue to pursue the projects I have become involved with, even if I know that they may not bear fruit until long after I have gone. There are days when these efforts can seem futile, when the effort involved outweighs the benefit accrued. But then there are other times when I see bright shoots wherever I turn. When I think about the relationships I have formed with men and women from the United States, or Britain, or Germany, or when I look around the offices of the Dialogue of Civilizations' Research Institute and hear people from around the world talking amicably in different languages and with different accents, I know that it is possible to substitute discussion and cooperation for aggression and chauvinism.

I was taught to survive, and I have survived. I hope that one day we will be able to say the same about mankind.

ACKNOWLEDGEMENTS

I t was my eldest son, Andrey, who first suggested that I write this book, and to him I owe thanks for the unstinting intellectual support that helped me to overcome my initial uncertainty. I would like to thank all those people whose love and devotion helped me to come through the toughest period in my life.

I am also very grateful to my friends who supported me during this work, and also to everyone at Biteback for their work on this book.

However, I would like to reserve my greatest thanks for all my colleagues, both those I have named in this book and the many I have not. There is very little I could have achieved in my life, without your talents, dedication, professionalism and support. There are some, too, to whom I owe my life – my gratitude to them knows no bounds.

INDEX

Russia *cont.*
  life expectancy 59
  living standards, Russian 7, 19, 57–8
  population of 9, 57–8, 147, 165–6, 249–51
  ports 94–7, 110, 134–7
  topography 148, 152, 153, 159
  tourism 146, 147, 148, 156, 164
  tsars 236
  'typical' outlook 6
  violence in 70, 91, 158
  weather 13, 154, 159
'Russia 1917. Images of the Future'
  (project) 258
Russian Olympic Committee 151, 163
Russian Orthodox Church Abroad 257n
Russian Railways 150–64, 166–70
  'best practice' 191
  control of 207–8
  infrastructure 143–5
  inspections 169
  international agreements 17
  leadership of 175–7, 194–5, 207
  Nevsky Express incident (2009) 213–17
  reforms 181, 188–97
  Sapsan line 17
  security measures 220
  smears against 219
  and Talgo 32
  tariff system 199, 200, 202, 202–5
  and Ukraine 87–8
Russo-Japanese War 182
Ryzhkov, Nikolai 189
RZD (Rossiiskie Zheleznye Dorogi) *see*
  Russian Railways

Sailors, Association of 136
St Petersburg
  demise of 57–60
  name change 206
  port of 94, 95
  US opinions 44
  violence in 119n
  water filters in 76

Sapsan line (Russian Railways) 17, 150, 197, 209
satellites 36
Saudi Arabia 228
Sayano–Shushenskaya power station 188
Second World War 47–8, 97, 183, 238
secret service agents 38–40, 91, 122–4
Semibankirschina (the seven bankers) 127
Serdyukov, Valery 98–9
Severomuysky Tunnel 150, 161
Shakhanov, Dmitry 92
shareholders 65–7, 74, 100
shipyards 91, 93, 130
Shoygu, Sergey 217
Shuvalov, Igor 203
Siberia 11, 12, 178, 188, 200
Siluanov, Anton 177
Sobchak, Anatoly 91, 95n, 121, 206
Sochi Winter Games (2014 Olympics) 143–4, 146–51, 164–7, 166
social networks 258
socialism
  ideas of 22, 35, 248
  values 6, 236, 240–41
Solzhenitsyn, Aleksandr 245, 246–7
South Korea 211–13
South Ossetia 86
Sovershayeva, Lyubov 99
Soviet Union
  end of 19, 24, 54–6, 67–8, 115, 178–9
  national republics 118n
  system 21
Spain 31–2
Spitak earthquake 47
statues, destruction of 68
Stiglitz, Joseph 111
Syria 220n
Systems
  banking 79, 135
  healthcare 12, 58
  judicial 125
  legal 88–9, 165